M000200352

WHAT RONNIE SUE KNEW

Recalling a Life of Love and Sparkle

STACEY TIRRO

These are my memories, from my perspective, and I have tried to represent events as faithfully as possible.

Copyright © 2021 by Stacey Tirro

All rights reserved. This book, or parts thereof, may not be reproduced in any form, stored in a retrieval system, or transmitted in any form by any means—electronic, mechanical, photocopy, recording, or otherwise—without prior written permission of the publisher, except as provided by United States of America copyright law.

What Ronnie Sue Knew, Recalling a Life of Love and Sparkle / Tirro, Stacey / Non-Fiction / Memoir

ISBN: 978-1-7362979-1-9 (paperback)

Edited by Shaundale Rénā
Cover artwork by Serena Hubert
Cover Design by Germancreative at fiverr.com

Printed in the United States of America for worldwide distribution.

First Edition

Published by Stacey Tirro
stacey.tirro@gmail.com
staceytirro.com

For Ronnie Sue and Stuart,

the ones who gave me life and taught me love.

Foreword

Houston, we have a problem. Although these were not the exact words spoken by astronaut Jim Lovell on Apollo 13, this erroneous quotation resonated with people across the globe in 1970. I would argue that the phrase, "Houston, we have a blessing," could easily apply to the arrival of Ronnie Sue in 2014. Although her "arrival" in the world was actually in 1947, any place Ronnie Sue occupied was a blessing to those around her.

I first met Ronnie at a diner in Rockland County, New York. I was excited to finally meet her because her daughter, Stacey, spoke so highly of her. If the axiom "the apple doesn't fall far from the tree" had any merit, I knew I was about to meet a very special person. Stacey Tirro is that special educator who delivers magic daily as she elicits greatness from students with a simple wave of her teaching wand. Stacey had told me, "My mother lights up a room." Well, Stacey was wrong. Ronnie Sue did not light up the room, she was the room!

When I first greeted her, I addressed her as Mrs. Roth; I never made that mistake again. It is difficult to put into words how initially speaking to someone for a short amount of time can make you feel as if you knew that person for a lifetime. Ronnie had the ability to put you at ease in mere seconds. She treated you as if you were the most important person in the room. Her words, gestures, and body language were absolutely genuine, and she had the gift of drawing you deeper into a conversation to learn more about who you really were.

There was no need for me to have the obligatory conversation about how special, respected, and talented her daughter was. Ronnie was well aware of the fact that Stacey inherited the "magic" gene. Ronnie had a way of looking into your eyes and smiling that made you feel both calm and confident at the same time. This is something you cannot teach; you have to live it.

I would never dare to say that I would be able to capture the essence of Ronnie Sue in writing. Somehow, her daughter was able to do just that. The grace, elegance, integrity, love, and courage that was Ronnie Sue is here for all to experience. From friendship, food and religion to career and family, the sparkle and panache of Ronnie Sue is pervasive throughout the pages.

During a phone call I had with Ronnie after she read my memoir, <u>Adversity Defeated: Turn Your Struggles into Strengths</u>, the intense emotion of her words and gratitude for my sending her the book were nothing short of surreal. How could someone so effortlessly utter words of thanks and encouragement in less than two minutes? Who could possibly know how to enter your heart so quickly and powerfully? Ronnie Sue Knew.

Cancer was no match for Ronnie Sue. Her attitude, grace, and dignity did not falter. Her determination, perseverance and strength were steadfast from diagnosis until the very end.

Ronnie Sue had cancer, but cancer never had Ronnie Sue. That is What Ronnie Sue Knew.

Marc Hoberman

CEO and Founder of Grade Success Education
#1 International Best-Selling Author
Creator of the Talk Show Lighting the Educational Flame

Acknowledgements

There are some important people to whom I would like to express my sincerest gratitude.

To Maria Palminteri-Arciniegas, my sounding board, and the one who always had my back at work whenever I had to drop everything and run to catch a flight to Houston. Your unwavering friendship made some extremely difficult times just a little more bearable.

To Marc Hoberman, my friend and inspiration, who helped me muster the courage to become an author. Your supportive positivity and guidance are greatly appreciated.

To Serena Hubert, my former student, a brilliant artist, and someone I am proud to call a dear friend. Thank you for creating such beautiful imagery to support the cover design.

To Shaundale Rénā, my editor, who guided me through the technical writing process while maintaining the loving message I was trying to convey. Thank you for helping me create the best version of this tribute to my mom.

To Richard Licata and Alan Brill, for giving Ronnie Sue the opportunity to delve into her passion for the law and recognize her immeasurable value in a law firm. To Lucille Barbato and Charles Spiegel, for enabling her to continue the second act of her career, embracing her and feeding her soul when she needed it the most.

To Anna, Lucy, and Jessica from Encompass Health, for treating Ronnie Sue like the VIP she was. Through the roller coaster of her last few years, you kept close tabs on her and gave her the opportunity for the best possible quality of life, despite the odds being stacked high against her.

To Victoria from Encompass Health Hospice, for her gentle guidance and loving support during some of the most difficult days I've ever experienced.

To Dr. Christine Lee at Memorial Hermann in Shenandoah, Texas, for bravely stepping in and saving Ronnie Sue's life. Because of you, we had a few more years to love and cherish her while she was on this earth.

To Lona and Sheila, for loving Ronnie Sue like a sister and for loving her family like your own.

To Christopher, Julia, and Sophia, my three most important people in this world. You keep me grounded and remind me every day what unconditional love is. You all make me a better person. I love you with every fiber of my being.

Contents

WHAT RONNIE SUE KNEW

Ronnie Sue in 2016

Introduction

Love doesn't die,
People do.
So, when all that's left of me
Is love,
Give me away.

~ Merrit Malloy, *Epitaph*

G rief is a maddening emotion. Sometimes it lingers under the surface of your skin, and your daily routines are familiar and regular. You almost forget that you have experienced trauma. Sometimes, at the very smallest sensation—a scent, a piece of clothing, a particular inflection in someone's voice, or even a random thought—the grief emerges, exploding out of its dormant phase, and it is enough to bring you to your knees. Even months or years later, the pain can be overwhelming, and even if it is for just a few moments, it is a not-so-gentle reminder that something or someone dear to you was taken away. When you lose your mom or dad, there is another level of feelings: discombobulation, emptiness, and the struggle of not quite knowing how to frame your own existence without them. The process of reframing your life is gradual, bumpy, and often uncomfortable.

Ronnie Sue was the eldest daughter of Morton and Mollye, two parents who seemed diametrically opposed in manner and personality, but whose hearts were forever intertwined. I am honored to be her child, the daughter of "Ronnie Sue, the southern Jew." In my lifetime, she was a New Orleans charmer transplanted temporarily in Yankee territory. To know her was to know love. If you were blessed enough to cross paths with her, to talk to her, to receive her counsel, you were so much the better.

I felt compelled to write this book, initially for selfish reasons. First, given how life is so unsteady and full of bad feelings, I wanted to put something out into the ether that was a reflection of love, something I could look to when I'm not feeling so great about the world. Second, I have a terrible memory. I am not one of those people who hears something once and commits it to her permanent mental hard drive— even the daily things I am supposed to remember, like when to pay the credit card bill, or picking up birthday cards, or what class am I teaching next. Let's just say, if I didn't have a calendar and reminders on my phone, schedules posted everywhere and a husband with a steel-trap memory, I'd be eternally lost.

Needless to say, when it came to remembering the snippets of stories about Ronnie Sue's past that she would tell me throughout the years, since they weren't essential to my daily routine, the details didn't always stick in my memory. Also, there were times when I would listen half-heartedly, distracted by whatever other mental chatter was also vying for my attention. I'd smile, thankful that she had shared her memories, and move on to the next thought. I'd always retain bits and pieces—a person's name, a specific event in time—and I always had the confidence that I would get more clarification when I heard the story again.

A third reason, and maybe the toughest to embrace, is acknowledging the different phases of grief you go through once you've moved past the initial experience of loss...like ground zero, one might say. Everyone encounters deep loss at some point in their lives, and how they advance through each phase depends upon various things. This memoir, while celebrating the lives of my mom and dad and how their influence impacted the trajectory of my life, also delves into the different facets of the grief I encountered when they no longer walked this earth. It was an intensely cathartic exercise that I look forward to sharing and hope that someone else may find some comfort reading these musings.

On what I had feared would be my last trip to be with Ronnie Sue, I knew it was unlikely that I'd have another chance to listen to her stories. I committed myself to spending whatever time we had left constructively, extracting as much history as I could in the few days after I arrived before her final decline. In truth, the stories may have holes, but they are the way she remembered and retold them the weekend before she passed. She would rest for long periods, wake up, sit up tall and be ready to talk, unlocking memories from her childhood, her marriage, her career, her experience as a parent, and beyond. Some stories I hadn't ever heard before, at least not in the detail she shared with me that weekend. "Cathartic" isn't quite enough to describe the feeling of having this opportunity to listen to and pen some of her last thoughts. I was mindfully appreciative of having this extended last chance to connect with Ronnie's past and present so that in the future, her spirit might live on indefinitely.

Which brings me to the less selfish reason for writing: everyone who knew Ronnie loved and adored her; many even worshipped the grace and kindness she spread daily. In the hours following her passing, so many condolences, prayers, and well-wishes flooded my social media, private messages, and phone calls. The outpouring of love and support was the most incredible tribute to the woman I got to call Mom, and I was further resolved to share the parts of her life and love that impacted me the most.

If you have a mom, had a mom, or recognize someone as a mother-figure, I think you will connect with the stories captured in these pages. If you knew my mom, this will resonate personally with you. If you never had the chance to meet her, this is a little introduction to an extraordinary woman who lived her life pragmatically, with simplicity mixed with a little bit of glitz. It is, in the simplest of terms, a love letter to Ronnie Sue Roth, the woman who graced this earth for almost seventy-three years, sprinkling her special stardust wherever she went. While it pains me to speak of her in the past tense, something I know I will never get used to and will always feel the weight of grief over, I do so with the knowledge that she lived her life on her own terms, unapologetically, gracefully and with great purpose.

Reflecting on Merritt Malloy's message to those of us who have been left behind...

> *So, when all that's left of me is love,*
> *give me away.*

I can't think of a better way to give Ronnie Sue away than to share her love with you.

What Ronnie Sue Taught Me

Children learn more from what you are than what you teach.
~ W.E.B. DuBois

Once I arrived in Houston and settled in next to her, I started thinking about everything I've learned from Ronnie Sue. Really, it was born out of reflecting on how I remembered her in the way she lived: What choices she made, how she dealt with different circumstances, and what made her content. As one lesson came to me, others soon followed. Very quickly, I had a very long list. I told her that I wanted to interview her, so I could capture whatever stories I could directly from her and who knows, maybe I'll write a memoir about her. She liked that idea. I started by reading this list to her. She smiled. I could feel the joy emanating from her. These topics were just the beginning of the many things I had to tell her in that precious last week.

This list was the key that unlocked Ronnie's brain, pouring out pages of accounts of a lifetime over that weekend, and the springboard for the creation of this book.

- *A mother gives her daughter unlimited love and cheerleading. Mom always had my back, no matter what.*

- *Sometimes, life looks better through rose-colored glasses.*

- *When your family needs it, drop everything, and take care of them.*

- *You have an unlimited reservoir of strength. It is always there when you need it.*

- *Take time to rest. The battle of life is exhausting.*

- *Women are natural leaders. When women embrace who they are and what they have to offer, they make everyone around them better.*

- *While you don't need a partner to survive, it can make life's journey easier to travel...and more fun.*

- *Loyalty to those you love lasts a lifetime.*

- *You do what you need to do to get something done but maintain your integrity and character as you go.*

- *You set the bar for achievement. Others may not strive to reach that bar, but that shouldn't stop you from setting it high.*

- *You don't have to agree with everyone else to be kind.*

- *Some things just make you mad. Even when that happens, you can still be respectful.*

- *Life is better with a dog. Dog hair in your space means you're loved unconditionally in the purest way.*

- *Use Windex to get stuck rings off swollen fingers.*

- *A little bling and glitz make life shine brighter.*

- *When you want something, giving up is not an option. However, you can decide it's not* worth the effort if you don't want it anymore.

- Be grateful for your life, even when life throws seemingly insurmountable challenges your way. Let the challenges teach you something.

- Pick. Your. Battles. You have just so much energy to spare. Use it wisely.

- Love the people your children choose to be with. They will love you back with ferocity.

- Play the long game; sometimes you need to pull back, give space, and move back in at a later time.

- If it's appropriate, pick up the tab.

- Take care of your skin. You can look good even when you've been through chemo.

- Find people with whom you feel a connection. It doesn't matter who they are, what they do, how much money they have, or their political affiliation. If their heart is *open to your embrace, give it fully and unabashedly.*

It gives me such joy to share not only her stories, but how these lessons became so emblazoned in my soul. Ronnie Sue didn't specifically sit me down to teach them to me; she just embodied all of these things. When I think of her, these are the things I associate with her being. It's now my job to recognize them, extract them, and share the wealth with the world.

A Southern Belle is Born

Home is a place you grow up
wanting to leave,
and grow old wanting to get back to.

~John Ed Pearce

In September 1947, Ronnie Sue Penner was born. She was the first of three daughters, all of whom were raised to be smart, sassy and have minds of their own. They lived on Derbigny Street in New Orleans and later moved to their big ranch-style house on Fleur De Lis Drive in Lakewood North, closer to Metairie. This is the house that I remember visiting on our lengthy family road trips. To my young eyes, it was a wonderland. Playing with my cousins, we'd move from room to room, exploring the knickknacks inside the drawers and closets of my mom's and aunts' childhood rooms—the remainder of the childhood stuff they had left behind when they moved into adulthood.

I remember being fascinated by the sense of my family's history in the old, creaky drawers of mom's wood dresser; I was in a place where my mom had grown up. Now, many years later, the next generation had a secret society where our code names were our names spelled backwards. We would move from room to room, exploring the nooks and crannies and play board games. I loved seeing my cousins, and since absence always made the heart grow fonder, I remember our playtime together as one of my sweetest childhood memories.

As the years passed, and we got older, the trips down south diminished. Our lives got busier, and the road trips were eventually replaced with summer programs, school activities and time with friends. Our regular exposure to Mom's family was lessened, which just became par for the course. We would see each other for special occasions, like my Bat Mitzvah, when everyone came up to New York to celebrate together. My mom, aunts and grandmother would re-create the bountiful dinner spreads and pictures would always be taken of the feast. I probably have more food pictures than people pictures from that time.

Ronnie Sue fondly recalled her childhood in New Orleans, Louisiana. She was well-liked, had friends, and even held on to a couple of them even through the end. Myra was her buddy from early on in grade school, who confirmed everything I already knew about my mom in one brief paragraph...

> *The major thing about Ronnie Sue was that she was born to be a nurturer. While other little girls were playing with dolls, she was always concerned about her friends, their home life, and their fears. She was a beacon of comfort at an early age. She had a constant smile. Her heart was good and kind. She laughed at my stupid jokes, talked about the names her daughters would have, and helped me steal snacks for our constant sleepovers. She was good, and I was bad. Since she was so tall at an early age, she looked older. I had her buy tickets for movies we had no business watching! She touched my life and many others because there was a constant smile in her heart.*

Growing up, I had a mental image of an idyllic place that Ronnie Sue had left behind. So many images were depicted in our home and would bubble to the surface—Mardi Gras posters, Fleur de Lis symbols, kitschy sayings about living and eating in NOLA (New Orleans, LA). Even though I grew up a Yankee, there was always a southern connection that permeated our life experience. I even slip into a slight southern drawl when talking to my family, and I have been known to insert the occasional "y'all" into casual conversations. When that happens, my husband and children look at me sideways and poke fun, but because of Mom, that small piece of my upbringing is always there. She made sure that just enough of the south would stay alive in New York.

Growing up, Ronnie Sue learned to value her family and thrived on those interactions. Despite the great distance between them once she moved away, her family was always near and dear to her heart. I remember hearing about numerous "cousins" over the years, and to be honest, I wasn't sure they were blood related since we didn't have a lot of extended family interaction. We had lived in New York since I was five, and I had to rely on the road trips we'd take to my grandmother's in the 70's and 80's to see any of the people she talked about. I remember pulling into the carport, the distinct smell of southern humidity, the thick blades of grass on her lawn, and the old side-by-side refrigerator that always had delicious food and Barq's red cream soda.

Ronnie was a rule follower and a people pleaser (something she certainly passed to me). In this way, she was very different from her mother. Ronnie often followed the path of least resistance, working hard to live up to expectations, to achieve, to become a better person, and to nurture everyone around her. Mollye was more of a bulldozer. She was also well-liked and had many friends, but if you got in her way, beware; she would always be the last one standing. The epitome of the strong matriarch, she wore that title like a crown. Like it or not, she was the boss and made sure everyone knew it.

I grew up knowing and loving my grandmother Mollye. Whenever we visited, she would make abundant dinner spreads to celebrate our arrival where we would see some of the immediate family. Dad would play the upright piano in the dining room, and we enjoyed time with the extended family. I remember having great fun during those trips, eating sno-balls doused with sweet, flavored syrup, shopping (my grandmother was obsessed with shopping), watching Mardi Gras parades (my grandmother rode on floats and threw beads and shiny doubloons to us), and cracking spicy crabs and crawfish on the newspaper spread over the kitchen table. Did I mention Barq's red cream soda? I think I did, but it was worth mentioning twice.

Since my grandfather died when I was so little, all I really had was my mom's loving memories of him. Mom regaled him as brilliant. *He could listen to a tv station, a ballgame on a transistor radio, and build a radio hifi electronic unit into a furniture console, all at the same time.* Ronnie Sue adored and worshipped her father.

*****

As I clicked at the keyboard, Mom's memory flashed back to her childhood, recalling the stories that she had remembered about her family. Her father, Morton, was born in 1924 in the Bronx to Chana and Sam, who divorced when Morton was young. Apparently, Chana had several husbands over the years.

> *Sam smoked cigars, drank whiskey, and ate dried salami. That was a meal for him. He actually came to New Orleans several times to visit and always brought each of the granddaughters a wrapped package of one hundred $1 bills each to go shopping. (WOW!) Sam was in the painter's union in Chicago, where he moved after they divorced. He was never a presence in Morty's raising, but he would appear from time to time to visit. We thought he was in the underground. He was the Hanukkah fairy!*

Our family's dirty little secret involved my great-grandmother. Throughout the years, I had heard references to her as "Chana the Hooker." One story Mom remembered very clearly about Chana was when her other grandmother, Miriam, flew her to New York for a holiday to celebrate her sixth-grade graduation...

That was an extraordinary experience; and I had an ear infection! (Oy!) We visited and stayed with my grandma Chana. When we walked in, I remember my grandma Chana being very nervous. We are standing in a hall. To the right is a kitchen. Chana says 'wait...I have food!' I sit down at a table in the hallway, and she brings me a bowl of SpaghettiOs— COLD, right out of the can. Then, from out of the living room, came two men. They had on pants with suspenders and guinea t-shirts. Bubbie grabs my hand and takes me into the dining room and down the hallway. She said, 'you sit right here till I come and get you.' Closed the door and then I heard nothing. I just waited. By the time she got me, the two yahoos were gone. We picked up like they never existed. Chana was also a card-shark and a money lender.

Needless to say, the women in my family always knew how to take care of themselves, for better or worse.

Despite my grandfather's challenging upbringing, Mom always spoke with reverent pride about her father. To her, he had a saintly way in which he treated his family and interacted with the world around him. Seems that he was adaptive, inventive, and always found a way to do what he felt was the right thing. For example, as a child, Morty had rheumatic fever so he couldn't enlist in military service. Instead, he trained homing pigeons for the military and worked in a munitions factory making bullets for the armed forces; this would be the extent of his service to our country, which he did proudly. Perhaps he was the influence that made her so patriotic; much of Mom's wardrobe had red, white and blue all over it.

On the other side of the family, Ronnie's grandfather, also named Sam, owned an antique refinishing factory in the French Quarter. When she was nine, he died of emphysema from exposure to the toxic fumes from the refinishing chemicals and glues he used every day. She remembered him fondly...

> *He was the most loving grandfather I could ever wish to have. 'Cooking spells'...this is how cooking came into my life (or didn't). One day he says, 'I'm a little hungry. See if Bubbie left anything for us to eat.' I climbed in his lap, went to the kitchen, and I see in the fridge a raw leg and thigh, a can of green lima beans, and a chopped-up tomato. Bubbie had gone out. In my eatery wisdom, I started to pan fry the chicken and flipped it a couple of times, thinking it was cooked. I put it aside and I got the little pot on the stove. I put in the lima beans and the tomatoes, and I put it on a slow cook. Then, I put the chicken and a couple of scoops*

of the beans and tomatoes into a bowl and proudly went to get my grandfather from the living room to the kitchen—time to eat! Well, you talk about a man of grace; he ate that raw chicken like it was made for a king. The lima beans were only half-cooked! He chewed them and then gave me such a big hug and said, 'that was DELICIOUS.' I can see the look on his face now. What an actor. No salt, no pepper, nothing! I was about eight years old. He asked if I could pick a few figs from the tree in the backyard. I came back with five huge figs for dessert. I almost killed him with raw chicken, but he had to have fresh dessert.

Sam loved to listen to opera. We would spend hours listening to the radio in the living room to these beautiful operas. I'd sit on his lap, and he'd ask me to clip his toenails. Proximity of unconditional love that made the relationship so memorable.

I think one of Mom's strengths, one of the messages I always received from her, was the blanket nature of her unconditional love. Clearly, she pulled this from her family, poured it into her friendships, and it informed her approach to parenting. To me, that was her key to success. From her perspective, it didn't matter if a child's work produced less-than-desired results; it was the effort that mattered and praise built confidence.

*****

My grandmother, Mollye, was born in 1925. A New Orleans socialite, Mollye was a go-getter and made friends wherever she went. She'd vacation in New York City and live it up. She was the child of Sam and Miriam, immigrants from Vilnius, Lithuania and Bialystok, Poland. Miriam was born in 1898. One of five children, Miriam and her sister Becky were sent to stay with relatives in Poland when her father, Ellis, brought the three boys to Ellis Island. Later, when Miriam was about thirteen, she and her sister followed on a steamship.

Young Ronnie Sue loved to watch her grandmother cook. Miriam hosted weekly poker parties. She also loved to work and always had a job in dress sales. Per Ronnie Sue, *she always got everything done; she finished things and was responsible.* That work ethic is a genetic trait that all of the women in that lineage share.

Miriam often took Ronnie Sue downtown in New Orleans, and they'd have fun together dining and shopping. *I felt very grown up when I was with my Bubbie. She was so effervescent. She looked like the grandmothers of the day, but a feisty one. I never had any fear when I was with my*

Bubbie. The women in our family also had spunk and professionalism emblazoned on our genetic code. I remember my great-grandmother, of course from a very different perspective. She was much older, and through the eyes of a young child, soft-spoken, frail-looking, and wrinkly. But I do remember how she and my grandmother would often clash; I'm guessing the mother-daughter relations of two independent firebrands made for some interesting conversations.

My great-uncle Leonard, Ronnie's uncle, was only twelve years her senior and like a big brother to her. He offered a little first-person family history. As a child, Leonard remembered his mother, Miriam, being out of the house fairly often. She made family dinners every night but spent much of her time out and focused on her community. A very social creature, the poker parties Ronnie Sue remembered were about hosting friends who were like family. Also immersed in Judaism, she went to shul every Friday and Saturday, and followed the Judaic philosophy of how to be a mensch (a person of integrity and honor) through doing mitzvot (good deeds). During World War II, she would have soldiers at the house for dinner every Friday night for a kosher meal, a welcome change from military rations. For Passover, she cooked a Seder dinner for 500 soldiers. When asked how she did it, she'd say "if you can cook for one, you get more food to feed more." Uncle Leonard said, "She had chutzpah. The woman was a hero beyond belief. She was trying to be a mensch; she took those things literally."

Though Mollye did follow her mother's philanthropic lead, the eventual clash between them arose out of a divergence in philosophy about family relationships. Miriam had specific ideas of what a good daughter should be and do. After Morty died, Miriam thought it would be appropriate for her to move in with Mollye. Mollye had different ideas, instead choosing to live alone for the rest of her life. Miriam, ever the busybody and assuming that personal boundaries were "flexible," thought she should be included in all of Mollye's social activities. Miriam felt she had the right to always be in everyone's business. Example: when at Leonard and Lidia's for a dinner visit with Lidia's parents, Miriam apparently made it a regular practice to look through all of their furniture drawers, as though it were her own house.

Apparently, this lack of boundaries, from time to time, contributed to clashes. Since Mollye ultimately had the final word, she set her boundaries and Miriam would eventually live in Woldenberg, a home for the aging, until she died at 93. Miriam apparently considered the nursing home a slap in the face, since she used to go there to pay social visits to the residents, and never understood why she couldn't live in

Mollye's big house. "They both thought they had the right of way," per Uncle Leonard.

Ronnie also developed a strong sense of boundaries and kept her personal life close to the vest. So much so that she spent her married life living far away from the home where she grew up. More on that later...

*****

The story of Mollye and Morty, as told by Mom, goes something like this. When Mollye was about twenty, she went with her mother to New York to visit Cousin Jenny, a maiden aunt who acted as the matchmaker. Jenny introduced Mollye to both Morton and "the guy who developed the Singer sewing machine." Of course, I have no idea who that person could have been, since the actual inventor died in 1875, but this tidbit was clearly an important piece of information in Mom's memory. No matter...the sewing machine guy lost out. Morty fell in love at first sight, and even though they lived over a thousand miles apart, they sustained a long-distance courtship, writing letters back and forth to each other. Morty eventually took the train to New Orleans to meet the family. They probably got engaged then and there.

Morty and Mollye were married in New Orleans at Beth Israel Synagogue in early 1946. She was a devoted fourth-generation member of the synagogue and would eventually serve as Sisterhood President and Board Member. However, in 1946, ever socially aware and business-savvy, Mollye decided they should change their last name, Penofsky, to Penner when they finally settled back in New Orleans later that year. Maybe she felt the name was too "ethnic-sounding" to be successful in business. Since her father, Sam, had fallen ill and needed Morty's help, they would be going into business in the deep south where Penofsky might hinder potential for success. Pragmatism would supersede religious pride in this case.

In the Bronx, Morty had owned a mini-factory where he made and sold women's fine leather and skin handbags and wallets. He sold that business when he moved down south so that he could help run his father-in-law's business, taking over when Sam died in 1956, even though it wasn't a business he enjoyed. When he had had enough, he switched careers to become a generic drug dealer as a sales rep for the Carroll Chemical Company. He ran his sales business out of the house to start. Louisiana was one of the few states then that allowed generic drug sales. It lasted a couple of years and when it became successful, he partnered with pharmacist Felix Welsh. He rented space from Welsh for a while to store inventory, then they went into business together, forming the wholesale pharmaceuticals company Penner and Welsh. Mollye kept the books, and he would later train her to take over the business with her brother, Leonard, and his wife, Lidia.

After Morty died, Mollye continued to run the business adeptly and was later named New Orleans Business Woman of the Year. I remember walking through the big Penner and Welsh storage facility as a child when my grandmother worked there. I didn't think anything of it then; my grandmother was the boss of everything, so it wasn't out of the ordinary from my perspective. Looking back, considering how rare it was for a woman to be the owner of a major pharmaceutical company, or any big business for that matter, I probably should have been more impressed.

*****

Morty was born Jewish but was not super religious growing up given his childhood environment. However, once they married, he and Mollye were committed members of Beth Israel synagogue in New Orleans, and he became an active leader in the religious community. Mom proudly remembered that he was also a 32nd degree Mason and had attained the position of District Deputy Master of the Masonic Lodge. His formal burial apron hung in a frame in Mom's room for years. Whenever she spoke of this part of his life, she felt it important to share that the inception of the Masonic Order was with the Knights Templar. Somehow, she always felt a connection to English history, and the mystique surrounding the Knights. Maybe her admiration of her father and his dedication to community service was a part of that, since the Freemasons organization was unitarian in nature and preached morality, charity, and obedience to the law of the land.

In keeping with the values of the Masons, Morty's service was always centered in helping the community to be brought together socially and spiritually; his personal mission was to act as a conduit between the main Christian and Catholic sects in New Orleans, and the Jewish synagogues. He wanted to educate the community about Jewish life and culture. Being a natural salesman, he'd go into areas of Louisiana, like the bayou, where people thought "Jews had horns" and worked to de-mystify people's perceptions about Jewish people. He founded Brotherhood Week which occurred once a year, where he brought together the different religious leaders to talk about religion and their impact on the community. The Shrine Circus was the biggest annual fundraiser of the Shriners, the social group of the Masons. Other fundraisers were to sign up to be in Mardi Gras parades and host big picnics in City Park and Audubon Park where Mollye would make her famous fried chicken and potato salad.

Looking at this from a 21st century perspective, I think my grandfather's dedication to bring people together was admirable. There always seems to be such divisions between people, deeply rooted in religion, class and culture. The courage he must have had to walk into the fire to try to change minds and hearts of those hardline prejudices - it is something most people don't have the constitution to pursue. Seems he made it his mission to poke through the mis-education and stereotyping of people in his community to try to develop a better understanding of who people really are. We could use more people like him nowadays.

Interestingly, as involved in Jewish life as she was, Mollye always kept her pragmatic wits about her. She kept kosher only for Passover...just in case the kids married into super-religious families. All bets were off the rest of the year; seafood was too important in the life of New Orleanians. Though they were conservative Jews, they belonged to the orthodox synagogue, where women and men were separated for the religious services. The idea always seemed so strange to me. While they embraced the orthodoxy of the temple and its cultural traditions while in shul, Mollye was a rebel at home, and it seems Morty didn't argue. Their life-choices suited them just fine.

Mom recalled her parents being financial savers, but not necessarily frugal. Morty gave Mollye whatever she wanted (within reason), but he was not particularly financially driven. He was a reasonable man, and he valued discussion, learning and teaching—qualities with which Mom strongly aligned herself. Ronnie Sue's worship and adoration of her father inspired her to follow his lead, finding ways to entrench herself in discovery and discussion. Not only did she love teaching what she knew, but she spent her life seeking knowledge.

She reflected on their joint parenting philosophy, which was rooted in discipline and respect. Individually, however, they had different styles of execution. Morty discussed things calmly; Mollye, being the authority on everything, yelled. Mom aligned herself more with Morty's, but when she got frustrated, you didn't want to argue when she raised her voice.

> *Daddy always built us up, Mollye resorted to the negative to get her point across. Daddy and I shared parenting styles. I felt safe because I had my father, and I knew from a very young age that he could be trusted with my emotions. I accepted from my mother who she was. My father could do no wrong; he was an idyllic parent. I actually went for counseling when he died. He was the strength—the mighty oak in my life. He impacted me in a great, great way. I still learned a lot from my mother. There*

wasn't anything she wouldn't do for her kids. The summer before I went to college was fun; mother made me my whole wardrobe. Hopefully, I was able to take the best of each of them and made my own parenting style.

You did, Ronnie Sue. You were the best.

I was fortunate to have met my grandfather as a small child. During Mardi Gras parades, he'd put me on his shoulders so I could see the floats. Mom recalled that he loved just holding me in his easy chair. Whenever I came into the room, he'd stop what he was doing, and I'd climb into his lap for a snuggle. He also snuggled with my cousin Michelle, the China doll itty bit of a child, with big opinions. Today, my "little" cousin, Michelle, has a PhD in Psychology and runs a successful private practice serving families in her community in Austin, Texas. Michelle is another example of the pedigree of professional women in our family.

My grandfather was diagnosed with colon cancer on my third birthday in 1974 and died three months later. From his diagnosis until the end, he remained in the hospital, and Mom stayed with him the whole time while my grandmother took care of me back at home. Sometimes, I think about the things that life throws at us. I've always struggled to find balance between dealing with the harsh realities of illness and death, while simultaneously celebrating the joys that life and family have to offer. Maybe navigating that balance is about finding the midpoint between the two and not getting too caught up in either one. I can only imagine the thoughts Mom tried to manage as she sat in his room, day after day, knowing she was right in the middle of that struggle.

Wanting to do whatever she could to make her daddy more comfortable, to cheer him up, Mom had a poster made of a three-year-old me that hung in his hospital room. As he neared the end, he slipped into a coma. I've heard this story from Mom many times, and she made sure to tell it to me again. The day he died, my mom, her sister, her Uncle Leonard, the Rabbi and Alvin Merlin (a surgeon and friend of Leonard's) were surrounding his bedside. Morty opened his eyes, looked everyone in theirs, pointed at my picture, and closed his eyes for the last time. Ronnie was 27. Her mighty oak departed.

With Morty gone, the significant, palpable tension between Mollye and my parents increased through the years. Once Mom married Dad and moved away from home, Mollye obsessed about Ronnie moving to New York. Apparently, Morty spent a lot of time working on Mollye, trying to reason with her and get her to move past her strong, irreconcilable feelings. *I got a magnificent letter from my daddy after we got married, apologizing for Mollye's behavior. She was depressed.*

Even after Ronnie grew up and started her own life, Morty's energy was spent protecting his baby and acting in her best interests. When we were cleaning out Mom's room, we came across a bag of old letters, including the one she talked about from her dad. I read that letter to Mom the day after she told me that story. It was remarkable to digest his words. You could sense the struggle he felt as he tried desperately to impress upon his wife that her treatment of her daughter was out of line. You could also sense that he felt badly for Mollye, that she couldn't get out of her own way to enjoy her daughter's relationship with a good man who treated her like gold.

*****

My grandmother was, if nothing else, a survivor. For 36 years after her husband passed, she was a successful businesswoman, lived a life of philanthropy, and had a brimming social calendar. She also beat cancer into the ground. When I was about 17, Mollye was diagnosed with thyroid cancer. My parents had given her a twenty-inch gold chain as a gift, and it was literally strangling her, prompting a visit to her endocrinologist. Blood tests revealed "unusual findings," so they decided to do an exploratory surgery. As soon as they cut her, the tumor expanded out of her neck. They immediately closed it up and he sent down a chemo doctor, which was apparently the completely wrong protocol to follow.

My aunt Judy, Mom's youngest sister who was a surgical nurse and the medical expert in the family, took over the case-making decisions. She took my grandmother to MD Anderson in Houston, Texas for an emergency visit where she was subsequently treated for more than twenty-five years. She had multiple surgeries to treat the cancer. In the first, they removed the tumor and took out part of her voice box. In another, they took the rest of the voice box and she had to live with a stoma in her neck so she could breathe. My grandmother, once blessed with the gift of gab, would be unable to speak without some sort of mechanical assistance.

It did not take long for my grandmother to adapt. Eventually she learned to speak with a Servox speech aid, which is a buzzing contraption with a small straw that you put in your mouth to create vocal sounds. Mollye spent years buzzing as she talked. Years later, she learned esophageal speech. Basically, she belched her way through a conversation. Nothing would stop her from conversing. My husband, Chris, recalls a frightful experience from early in our marriage during a family visit to New Orleans. We were all packed in the car, Mollye at the wheel. She was giving us a tour of the garden district and Chris was in the front passenger seat. Ever the chatterbox, she'd have one hand on the wheel and talk with her Servox as she drove and played tour guide. Every so often, she'd point to a home as she gave us the history behind it. Chris looked back at me with panic in his eyes; there were no hands on the steering wheel! Welcome to Mollye's world.

Mollye was...opinionated. She didn't mince words and her inner filter never fully developed. If she didn't like you, she made you uncomfortably aware of it. This made for years of stress for Ronnie when it came to my dad. Despite his best efforts, he never seemed to be able to live up to Mollye's expectations *and* he had taken Ronnie away from the family. I think Mom's way of coping was to stay away. If she couldn't make the situation better, it was best to keep the distance between them.

Mom's quiet rebellion in making her choice vexed Mollye, who became increasingly aggressive towards my dad as the years passed. The final straw happened after he died. When we were sitting Shiva, the rabbi asked everyone in the room to take a turn to speak about Stuart. When it was Mollye's turn, she admitted, "I have nothing to say about him." That was one of the most tragic and uncomfortable moments I'd ever experienced. Mom recalled, *that's when she made a fool of herself.*

The shiva incident cemented the rift between Mollye and Ronnie Sue, and while we still had occasional visits from Mollye when she was traveling, their relationship was certainly damaged. Many years later, when she came up for a visit, Mollye made an admission to Mom in a Walmart parking lot: she was jealous and angry that Dad took her daughter up north; she had always wanted to live there herself. She didn't because her father was sick, and she knew she would have to take over the antique business in New Orleans. Really, she wanted to "be a star" in New York. This revelation was such a shock to Mom's system because of how petty it felt for a mother to treat her daughter's family that way. In the end, according to Mom, it was an admission that was too little, too late. Not an apology for poor behavior— just a "matter of fact."

As Mom told me this story, I could see her struggle. In her mind, that kind of admission went against the Judaic code of raising children, which she thought always taught parents to want and strive for more for their children than they had. The balance of wanting for yourself versus wanting for your children seemed way off to her when it came to her mother. I don't think this balance was necessarily written in the Torah or hashed out by the great Rabbis, but I like that Mom felt that way. As I see it, Ronnie chose to live her life in a way that balanced her father's empathy, good humor and nurturing of others with her mother's resilience and fortitude; as Ronnie Sue had hoped, the best of both parents.

Despite the family tensions and unapologetic personal slights, most of my childhood memories of Mollye were good. I remember shopping with her on our trips to New Orleans, watching her make gumbo and rice (and devouring it), and tearing apart seafood on her round wooden kitchen table. She loved her family, but it had to be on her own terms. Her zest for life was admirable and her strength second to none. After a long, prosperous life, Mollye died at 86. She was buried on Ronnie Sue and Judy's birthday.

Stuart Barry

***I've said it before, but it's absolutely true:
My mother gave me my drive, but my father
gave me my dreams.
Thanks to him, I could see a future.***

~ Liza Minnelli

Stuart Barry Roth was a Jersey boy, born in 1941, to Adelaide and Sam. Unlike Ronnie, he was raised in a more traditional, orthodox Jewish home. Adelaide was a public schoolteacher and children's choir director; Sam was a butcher.

Stuart was very interested in sports and was quite an athlete in high school but was also an extremely talented musician, learning the drums and piano at an early age. He started playing the family's baby grand piano in the house at four or five years old. He learned how to read music in his early lessons, but eventually abandoned written music when he got older and simply played by ear. It was an extraordinary talent that amazed me, and it always served him well as an entertainer. In high school, he was the drummer for an event band he formed with some high school buddies and played for local events and parties for extra cash.

He graduated from Cranford High School in 1959 and went to University of Alabama for one year on a full track scholarship. After the second semester, he was invited to play football under head coach Bear Bryant, but alas, it was not meant to be. After his first year away at college, Adelaide implored Stuart to come home. My grandmother was somewhat of an over-controlling parent who tended to see the negative side of events. Though she loved her family, she always seemed to find fault with things and often used guilt to get her way. In her opinion, "Jewish boys don't play sports." (Ouch!) Neither did he need to go away to college, nor did he have to be so far away from home. Subsequently, he dropped out at the end of his first year and spent the next year or two trying to figure out what to do afterward. Dad supposedly played baseball with the Yankee farm team in the summer of 1960. From 1960-1962, he worked, played gigs with his band, and tried to make a new plan.

When I think of my dad, I think of a tall, hefty man with a big belly and a mop of curly brown hair. I remember him munching on black licorice and pretzels while watching a baseball or football game, but never participated in any sports activities. As a kid, I never really knew that he had any significant athletic talent. When I was older, we would go for long power walks on the school track—certainly a middle-aged weight-loss effort on his part—and he would walk for miles. Maybe the memory of walking away from sports was painful for him, and this was also a way he chose to reflect.

He eventually enlisted in the Air Force Reserves and served for seven years. In June 1962, he reported to Sheppard Air Force Base in Texas, Airman 3rd Class. He finished flight traffic specialist instruction—114 hours at Tinker Air Force Base in Oklahoma and was promoted to Staff Sergeant. Dad was a Loadmaster; one of his duties was flying the bodies of fallen American soldiers back home from South Asia. Mom recalled a story about the first time he flew the mission. During the flight, he heard moaning from the coffins. Apparently, the change in altitude and pressure affected the bodies and made them groan—a creepy detail that made for a good party story.

While he served, Dad often got requests from Adelaide's friends to get Rosenthal China from Germany. He would shop in town, get it on the cheap, and have it shipped back stateside. I'm guessing these were the families of German Jews who were yearning for something from back home.

After Mom and Dad were married, he went to Essex County College in Newark, New Jersey and received his Associate

Degree in Business Administration, six months before I was born. He continued to play music gigs, but switched to the piano, since drums had too much gear to schlep from place to place. Mom thought the band was an escape for him; it was something he truly enjoyed, he made some money, and he could show off something he had a great talent for. Since Adelaide was a musician herself, I'm thinking she felt this was an activity that was more suitable for her son.

Sam, on the other hand, was more relaxed and fun-loving. He also loved family but was less of a disciplinarian; he left that to Adelaide. Stuart got his affable personality from his dad. Though he had made goals for himself early on, many were objectives of which Adelaide didn't approve. Like Ronnie, Stuart's mother issues were intense. The main difference is that he didn't move a thousand miles away to ease the tension. The personality friction over the years challenged his self-worth, which seemed to be a root cause for all sorts of problems for him in adulthood. However, Ronnie Sue provided quite the opposite feedback than his mother. She was a break from the negativity and was always supportive of his goals. *I think that's why we had a good marriage. No matter what he wanted to do, I'd say 'let's go try it.'* The attraction between them was strong to begin with. Their shared experience with over-controlling, dominant mothers probably connected them further, and it seems they were each other's escape from that reality.

Dad eventually found his way in the jewelry business. I remember he always had a tall, black, rolling case full of a line of jewelry samples that he would show to businesses and write orders to supply their stores. Mom told me how vast Dad's talents were in his field: very creative instincts, an innate sense of how to present something, and the ability to design jewelry to fit the fashion of the day. Over the years though, he struggled. Even though he was a fabulous salesman, there was something missing about his business sense. He had an idealistic way of looking at things, but it wasn't always practical, and that conflict proved to make for a difficult career path. This probably went poorly with any authority figures he clashed with. He didn't see it as an issue, but according to Mom, it did affect his level of achievement because he felt that he could have been more successful had people just listened to his ideas. Unfortunately, moving to a higher level of business success always seemed to elude him. He had big ideas but couldn't always get the buy-in from others to get things off the ground. This regrettably followed him throughout most of his life, impacting his work, his volunteering, and sometimes their marriage. Mom saw it happening and she tried to help steer him; sometimes it worked and sometimes it didn't.

Despite his struggle with business, Dad was extremely well-liked. His personality was larger than life. He walked into a room, and he could make anyone who was having a bad day turn it around and think they were in the greatest place on earth; this was one of his gifts. His bellowing laugh was infectious, and his bear hugs always made me feel secure. My friends always loved my dad. He was a comedian, forthright, and never let people forget how much he loved and adored the women in his life. And of course, anyone lucky enough to be in our house when he played piano was entertained by his incredible musical talent.

When I was in high school playing the flute in the marching band, Dad found out there had been a Band Parent's Booster Club years before I got to high school and for whatever reason, it disbanded. He wanted to get more parents involved (like Pete and Ivonne, now my wonderful in-laws) to help the students. He was a great organizer and worked tirelessly to solve the problems he saw. He'd discuss his ideas with Mom, then move forward. On my fourteenth birthday, there was a blizzard. It was also the Homecoming game of my freshman year, which was not canceled. Rather, the team played and thus, so did the band. We played our halftime show with frozen fingers and ended our routine kneeling in the snow. Dad realized that parents had to step up and do a little more for their freezing kids and came up with a brilliant idea. Mom recalls:

> *He said, "I'll be right back." Twenty minutes later, he comes back with these containers of hot chocolate for the kids. He gathered all the students into the bleachers, who he had asked to brush the snow off the benches (for ours and the opposing team as well...because it was the right thing to do), and he brought the hot chocolate to each of our students. They were so grateful. That was a wonderful quirk about him. We never discussed little plans; he wanted to surprise me. These are the things that parents need to do to help their kids. Children were his heart and soul. I just went along for the ride. I had a ball.*

I remember that game and the hot chocolate. It also made me a little bit famous amongst my peers; my parents were the ones who brought the hot chocolate treat. As a child and young teenager, I worshipped my dad like my mom worshipped hers. He was fun and musical and was always game for a bear hug. He taught me how to ride the big red Toro lawnmower, how to throw a baseball (the most we did in the sports realm was to enjoy our baseball catches together in the yard), how to drive, and ultimately led me to the career I've spent most of my adult life cultivating. We had some difficulty as I grew into adulthood—the natural process of his little girl growing up didn't sit well with him—but I never questioned the love my father had for me. In his own way, he helped to set me up for the rest of my life.

Ethics of My Mother

Which is the right path for man to choose for himself?
Whatever is harmonious for the one who does it, and harmonious for mankind.

~Ethics of our Fathers

The traditional practice of religion, much to my dad's dismay, was not something that stuck with me past my Bat Mitzvah. As much as he tried to carry it forward throughout his household, he had also encouraged me to pursue my own interests, which sometimes flew in the face of my connection to spirituality. While both of my parents set the foundation for leading good Jewish lives, the traditional nature of Judaism was much more important to Dad than it was to Mom. This did create some serious conflict, particularly as I got older and was seriously dating someone who was not Jewish.

Where Dad valued the traditional details of going to shul with the family and celebrating holidays together, Mom's take on Judaism, particularly as she got older, was more of a 30,000-foot perspective.

> *I believe that our lives evolve based on God's recognition of what needs to be. That's about as religious as you're going to get from me. I see Heaven as a place to be able to see one's life in the best possible way.*

Ronnie Sue's upbringing in a conservative Jewish home, where they attended orthodox services, set the foundation for how she would present religion in her home as an adult. Learning how to keep kosher for Passover proved to be a valuable skillset for her, and we did keep the kitchen "kosher-style" for most of my childhood. But, for those visits to Fleur de Lis Drive, seafood was bountiful in Mollye's kitchen. I remember one of the first meals when would arrive from our two-day road trip was crawfish, shrimp and crabs spread out over newspaper on the kitchen table. I remember how the spiciness of the Old Bay seasoning made my lips burn as I tore apart the crabs and twisted the tails off of the crawfish, dipping them into homemade cocktail sauce and crunching on Ritz crackers. The lessons Mom learned were that the rules could be adjusted according to how one wanted to live their life. If it meant enjoying a table full of crustaceans or devouring a bowl of Gumbo over rice or inhaling a fried oyster po'boy, so be it. When your mother is the boss of everything, you don't really question her life choices; you go with the flow. Especially when it is delicious.

Socially, Mom's parents were strong leaders in the Jewish community in New Orleans. The tenets of philanthropy, service and education were all modeled daily, and Mom followed suit as a volunteer in arts education.

While Mom was not traditionally religious at heart, she had her own sense of spirituality. She spoke of a book called *Ethics of the Fathers*, a companion piece to the Mishnah, the first set of oral Jewish laws in the Talmud. It is a collection of statements expounding upon the ethical principles attributed to the original Rabbis of the General Assembly. According to the book, these Rabbis received the Torah (the written laws of God) through an unbroken chain of transmission—from God to Moses at Sinai, to Joshua, to the Elders, to the Men of the Great Assembly. They were responsible for interpreting the Torah. With the passing of each generation, the Torah was often read and interpreted in different ways, each Rabbi focusing on specific angles they felt were most important in the study of Torah.

Mom's spirituality and morality operated under the premise that she would always follow the path that led to her doing the most amount of good. If her intention and action meant people were treated with kindness and respect, that was the path she chose to follow. I think it's fair to say she took the offerings from *Ethics of the Fathers* that her parents passed to her through their personal philosophy and promoted the general principles that made the most sense to her worldview. I liken it to picking the sweetest cherries in the orchard. Why spend your energy on the sour ones?

Mom definitely had strong opinions about how to live her life, but she was also an advocate for discussion and learning from others. Her life decisions weren't made with the Torah in the forefront; she wasn't a chapter and verse kind of person. I think the foundation of her upbringing, particularly Morty's influence, was in the back of her mind as she carried on day to day. Mom wanted to always contribute her thoughts and actions to the world in a positive way. What is right about a decision? Who will be happy?

Ronnie Sue always took into consideration other people's wants and needs when making decisions. I think this is something I picked up from her. Sometimes it takes me a long time to land on a decision because I'm constantly weighing the pros and cons of who it will impact and how. What was interesting is that I was never really privy to Mom's ongoing thought process itself; she often kept that to herself. Rather, I saw the outcome and impact of her decisions on others. Largely, the impact was beneficial, and her treatment of others was kind and embracing. Whatever she chose, she wanted to offer a useful, positive, boosting service to the people she loved.

The concept of promoting and supporting "goodness" wasn't reserved just for the outside world but was applied in our home as well. I remember growing up that I always wanted to do the "right thing." This was a direct reflection of what my parents modeled for me. I was a rule follower who was encouraged to pursue my passions, which were wholeheartedly supported by both of them. The only caveat to that emerged when I started dating a boy who was not Jewish in my senior year of high school. This was where my parents' personal philosophies seemed to diverge. My father was still an active member in the synagogue, despite my choice to put my attention into other things after being Bat Mitzvah. He would regularly try to get me to accompany him to Shabbat services, but as I got older, there were other things filling my calendar. I was busy with school events, rehearsals, work and my developing social life. My mom, ever the busy bee, would help counsel my dad when he lamented that his family wasn't going with him. That counsel would likewise extend when my relationship with Chris shifted from platonic to romantic.

Chris was a sophomore when I entered high school. He was kind, gentle and welcoming. He was one of the people in the band who introduced me to his group of friends when I was a freshman. When my parents became involved in the Band Parents Booster Club, they worked closely with Chris' parents. They knew Chris to be a sweet, smart, responsible young man who was a good friend to their daughter. When he went to college in the fall of my senior year, we started dating. I think the knowledge of this threw my dad for a loop. In his mind, I was getting ready to go to college, set up the skills for a career in the performing arts, and figure out a life for myself. Then, I should find a nice, Jewish boy to spend that life with. Seeing this relationship blossom and grow throughout my college experience was not something Dad was prepared to accept, no matter how good I thought it was for me.

In my last year of college, Dad realized that this relationship was something serious. We had survived long-distance dating throughout college, and the fact that Chris was not Jewish was still a major roadblock in my relationship with my dad. We had spent years growing apart, unable to talk about it because it was too uncomfortable, and we were both emotionally too dug in to be able to come to any real understanding about the situation. He really liked Chris as a person; he had known him for years through our friendship in high school. Chris was "good people from good stock," but this was superseded by Dad's concern that I might eventually marry someone out of the faith.

Ronnie Sue did her level best to alleviate his concerns. In that way, Mom took a cue from Morty, who had pressed Mollye hard to be more accepting and empathetic towards Ronnie's relationship with Stuart. She knew how much it hurt and didn't want to see me endure the same stress that they had over the years. She shared her memory of conversations with Dad where she implored, *this has nothing to do with religion and everything to do with a relationship that has the possibility of being very strong. It doesn't make sense.* Again, if an argument didn't make sense to her, she could not support it, especially when it came to her kid. Mom wasn't the type to blindly follow her husband's lead. She would have spent years working to convince him of the good things about the relationship, had she had the chance: the fact that Chris and I adored and were good to each other and that he would be an excellent partner to support a life and family together. To her, my relationship with a good person made good sense. Trying to stop it because of religion did not.

This is an example of the cornerstone of exercising her philosophy on spirituality and parenting—what will be best for the child. In this light, it was probably the greatest divergence from her mother's behavior. It was never about her personally; she always gave deference to what she saw was best for me, and she largely let me lead the way, being there as a support and a guide. She didn't get hung up on the traditional aspects of Judaism. She was happy to participate as a family and supported my dad's more traditional desires while I was growing up, but her personal philosophy ultimately followed the path of *what will be, will be*. She saw good things as serving a purpose in life. She respected my age, observed how Chris and I behaved during dating, and appreciated everything about the relationship.

Ronnie Sue left it to the universe (and to us) to decide what would happen in the future, and I am thankful that she did. Sadly, I am often left to wonder if Mom's influence would have eventually chipped away at Dad's philosophy on religion and family. I'd like to think so. I am forever grateful to her for providing a protective shield around us so that we were free to allow our relationship to develop naturally. Chris and I have a bond that has matured and strengthened for more than thirty years. We are raising two incredible women who are carrying on the goodness and strengths of their Nanny and Papa Stu. Now that she is reunited with Dad, I'd like to think they are celebrating our marriage and the family we have created together.

Ronnie Sue Grew Up

I'm a woman,
Phenomenally.
Phenomenal woman,
That's me.

~ Maya Angelou

On both Derbigny Street and Fleur de Lis Drive, Ronnie Sue enjoyed a happy childhood. There, she started her busy path of social engagement. In high school, she loved athletics, playing on various teams, and proudly sported a crooked pinky finger from a softball injury she sustained. In B'nai B'rith Girls, she attended monthly meetings, fundraisers, and cotillions. She graduated Alcee Fortier High School in 1965 and attended LSU Baton Rouge for a year and a half.

She left college after her third semester to work for a year as a legal secretary for an attorney named John Pisa before getting married and moving away from home. My Uncle

Leonard shared with me that Mr. Pisa perished in a French Quarter altercation. Apparently, he rubbed the wrong person the wrong way and was stabbed to death. I'm sure that was difficult for Ronnie Sue to take; in one of my dad's letters to her back in 1968, he referred to her having recurring stomach pain and asked how Mrs. Pisa was doing.

I'm guessing Mom had a hard time processing the whole event. Historically, she tended to get very close to the people she worked for, nurturing them like she did everyone else. When she respected her bosses, she poured her whole being into her work and only wanted to learn more from them. The attorneys Ronnie worked for, starting with Mr. Pisa, lit a spark in her that lasted her entire lifetime.

*****

Living far away from her family, though by choice, was tough on Ronnie Sue at times. I would imagine it was especially hard to be away from the familiarity of southern living and her younger sisters. Even with such distance between them, I remember there being an almost magical quality about their collective relationship. The Penner girls talked on the phone regularly and when they were together, it seemed like no time had passed.

For nine years, Ronnie Sue and Cheryl were the only kids in the house, and as many siblings do, they endured some growing pains. Cheryl was two years younger than Ronnie. Apparently, Ronnie was quite the bossy older sister and Cheryl, being the strong-willed second child, did not take too kindly to that. Cheryl recalled the big red chair that was the seat of choice in the living room. On Saturday mornings, it was a race to see who got to sit in the chair and Ronnie, being bigger and faster, always beat her younger sister to it. One day, when Ronnie ordered a smoldering Cheryl to make her eggs for breakfast, she complied as she stewed. Her patience was pushed a little too far; from the kitchen, she hurled a fork at her older sister. Luckily, it was a miss, but the message was sent loud and clear. She would not tolerate being pushed around. Today, all is forgiven, and the beloved big red chair sits in Cheryl's home.

On her eleventh birthday, Ronnie Sue recalled receiving the *best birthday present ever.* After imploring her very pregnant mother to wait an extra two weeks to give birth to her baby sister (to which Mollye replied, "are you kidding me?") Ronnie got a phone call that confirmed her wish was granted. She now had a living doll to play Mommy with. *It was the most fun. She became the light of my life. Judy was my little baby.* She took pride in playing Mommy to her youngest sister.

Mollye used to let her take the baby on the bus to Audubon Park. One day, Ronnie took Judy to see "The Sound of Music" in the movie theater. It occurred to Ronnie that her little sister looked exactly like the character Gretl and said, *Look Judy! There you are! Gretl!* Ronnie called her relationship with Judy *angelic...magical.* A fun fact that Ronnie shared, they were so connected that they had the same number of cavities at the same age growing up.

Judy grew up calling Mom Nonnie Nue because she couldn't pronounce her R's. Mom had a little purple satin pillow that Judy had made her with "Nonnie Nue" embroidered in gold. I returned it to her at the funeral. In one of Judy's last conversations with Nonnie Nue, she lovingly expressed, "I feel like I grew out of your hip."

For all intents and purposes, once Ronnie Sue got married (Judy was nine) and moved away, she split from the family. She admitted that she got a little lazy with keeping the relationships up from home while raising her family up north. Cheryl had moved her family from Dallas to New Jersey for a few years when I was young, and the elder sisters got a little closer as the families got together more regularly, but when Mom moved to Texas in retirement, their relationship truly blossomed. Absence made the heart grow fonder...Cheryl was finally able to spend quality time with her sister for good. (No more fork throwing.) With Judy only a few hours away, they were all able to enjoy each other's company in person more often, travel together, and renew the sisterly bond that had been forged over a lifetime.

Right after Ronnie passed, Judy texted me:

In my mind's eye, when she stopped breathing, her brilliant essence peeled away from the body in the bed and spent some time caressing each of you. That beatific smile... I'd like to think that her soul, in its ability to transcend time and space, would take a little time to shower some love over her sisters as well before making its way into the great unknown.

Pook and Pookie

Love letters straight from your heart
Keep us so near while apart
I'm not alone in the night
When I can have all the love you write

~ Heyman Edward, *Love Letters*

The bag of letters I found as we were going through Mom's stuff during her last few days was such a gift— full of old letters, pictures, and mementos of her early life. It was a gold mine, really...an extended series of snapshots into a world that I was never privy to growing up. The most amazing discoveries were all the letters my dad had written to her during their long-distance courtship. Almost daily, they would scribe sentiments of adoration, report on the mundane, and delve into their hopes and fears as they approached their wedding day. They had the mush and sap of new love, mixed with the responsible practicality of planning for "adulting," each section weaving together the delicate intricacies of Dad's inner psyche. The best part was his pet name for her—Pook. I remember growing up how they'd occasionally call each other Pookie. I always made fun of them for that. Now, I think it's the sweetest thing.

What was most interesting was seeing the reflection of my dad's personality—the things I remember about him growing up, revealed in the early history of their relationship. As he scribbled (unlike Ronnie Sue, penmanship was not one of his strengths), he revealed the things he struggled most with: an overly dominant mother, his issues with authority figures, his deep-seated fears of failure, and his overwhelming desire to be a "mensch." He even talked about seeing an analyst to help him unpack the many years of troubles he had endured, trying to dig into his past in order to pave the way for a better future. It was admirable, his tenacity and commitment to setting up a strong foundation for a successful marriage. I'm sure he wanted to do things differently from what he experienced in his own upbringing, as many young people do as they separate from their parents' influence. Bottom line, Stuart wanted to be a better man for Ronnie.

At first, it seemed to me to be out of character; I don't remember my dad ever entertaining the idea of therapy as I was growing up. But as I thought about it, I got the impression that he was doing it, perhaps at the behest of his future in-laws, to get his head in the right place. A self-admitted rebel with authority issues, he seemed to realize that to be the best husband and eventual father, he'd need to get to the root of his hang-ups. I think he wanted to model himself after his future father-in-law: a successful businessman, devoted to his wife and kids, adored by his children, and the "mensch" Stuart wanted to become. Despite his future mother-in-law's dominating tendencies that mirrored those of his own mother, he complied with whatever requests they made before they gave their blessing to him to take their eldest daughter away.

*****

Ronnie and Stuart met in New Orleans during Thanksgiving of 1966. He was working at Service Merchandise for his uncle Irving, who trained Stuart in the jewelry business. He was sent to jewelry shows in New York and Irving hoped he would stay to eventually run the business. Ronnie Sue came home from college one weekend and Cheryl was supposed to babysit *Sharon's three crazy kids.* Sharon was Uncle Irving's daughter, Stuart's cousin, whom he was staying with while he worked at the store. Cheryl couldn't babysit, so she asked Ronnie to cover for her. Stuart came home from work at 11 p.m. and started playing the piano, probably to impress Ronnie. Needless to say, she *was* impressed. He asked her out for that Saturday night, and that was the beginning of their courtship.

Like Morty and Mollye, they literally fell head over heels for each other. She admitted that once her love affair with Stuart began in the fall of 1966, she transferred to LSUNO in January of 1967 to be closer to him. She wanted to be distracted by the love of her life. Needless to say, Mom was distracted indeed. I found one of her college report cards. Let's just say, Stuart was a bad influence on Ronnie's academic career. According to one of Dad's last letters to her before their wedding, they had about three months together before he moved back up north, where they would spend the next year-and-a-half managing their relationship from a distance.

In June, Stuart paid a visit to New Orleans from McGuire Air Force base with a big surprise—a marriage proposal. Ronnie was a bridesmaid for her roommate, Raenell. Fun fact that Ronnie shared: Raenell's uncle was Justice Abraham Fortas of the Supreme Court, who was also at the wedding. Stuart came to her hotel room with the bridesmaids and proposed with a two-carat round diamond right then and there. (Everyone else, including the bride, knew about the proposal.) Ronnie performed her duty as a bridesmaid with a big, shiny rock on her hand. *It was niiiiice.*

The flurry of letter writing continued over the next year. They set their wedding date for June 30, 1968; the countdown to nuptial bliss had begun. They wrote about everything under the sun. Often, Dad would ramble in a stream-of-consciousness brain dump, scribing page after page, almost as though he was channeling Ronnie's presence when his pen hit the paper. He seemed genuinely interested in the wedding plans, which Mollye was largely controlling, and would check in to see what gifts were coming in. He talked about the acquisition of their bedroom set, the new television he purchased (which he loved), and his meticulous musings of their current financial state. He was nothing if not present and attentive to the planning of their future together. For Stuart, their relationship seemed to mark the beginning of a brand-new, happy life.

My parents continued their lives apart, planning for their future. As if that weren't dramatic enough, the current events of the day would cause some nuptial stress. On January 23, 1968—six months into their engagement—The USS Pueblo, a Navy intelligence vessel, was captured by the North Koreans in international waters. At that time, Dad was still active in the Air Force Reserves and had to report to base for four months at a time. He was notified that he would be activated to go on a long-term assignment in North Korea.

Wedding invitations had gone out and Ronnie was understandably worried. To put her mind at ease, Morty said, "Don't worry. We'll have a wedding with or without him." Of course, there was no way my dad would miss saying "I do" to his dream girl. The night before his medical checkup, he may have over-eaten. (Maybe twenty packets of sugar was too much?) Based on his blood work, they decided to keep him on the base for the remainder of his assignment.

My parents were married on a Saturday night. To celebrate the wedding, in line with southern tradition, there were eight hosted luncheons and showers in honor of Ronnie Sue and Stuart. According to southern tradition at the time, *all your friends throw a party for you—multiple parties by multiple people, handkerchief luncheons. The Sunday after the wedding, someone threw a brunch. Stuart didn't want to go; he was so tired, but I made him go.* I'm pretty sure my Yankee father couldn't wait to get away from the hullabaloo and just get on with being married to his dream girl.

Mollye, being a *control freak*, had planned and picked out everything, including her wedding dress, which incidentally, I also wore at my wedding. *Oh God, that was an event—one of the most exciting days in my life. I didn't make a decision!* I asked her what some of her most memorable moments from her wedding day were:

Walking around your daddy three and a half times and looking at him. He had a tear in his eye. I had never seen him cry... Walking down the aisle. It was so long, and I had such a long train...The party was great. We had a really great time.

When unencumbered by the stress of life, my parents really enjoyed each other's company. Even with their personality quirks, they adored each other. If they could have lived in a bubble, without the controlling mothers and financial pressures, I think they would never have had a fight. Even as she was nearing her end, Mom spoke adoringly about him. Stuart was the one true love of her life.

After the nuptials were over, Ronnie Sue changed into the post-wedding suit Mollye had made for her and left the affair a "Sadie, Sadie Married Lady." The weekend after, they packed up and moved to Cranford, New Jersey, where Stuart had spent the last few months setting up their humble abode and started their adventure together. They spent their honeymoon week in Manhattan, and upon their arrival at the Plaza Hotel, they opened the room door only to find two separate twin beds. This was an unacceptable situation. Stuart, ever the fixer, quickly pushed them together. Problem solved. That's how he worked...if there's a problem, there's always a solution. All week, they traipsed around

Manhattan and did all the touristy things: Broadway shows, walked the streets, and saw the sights. That was the first time since the sixth grade that Mom had been to New York— luckily, a far cry from her experience at Grandma Chana's.

The newlyweds had some challenges to surmount early on. Stuart was still committed to the Air Force Reserves and had to report back to base at the end of the honeymoon week, so Ronnie temporarily lived with Adelaide and Sam. Since she was Jewish and kept kosher, Adelaide found her a suitable match for her son... For the moment.

Mom said Dad wanted kids immediately, but she convinced him to wait a little bit. She wanted to make sure he was settled with work before expanding the family. My dad was always very concerned about finances. Between that and some of the ongoing issues he was working on, Mom knew it was better to be patient. She had always worked in law offices, and she knew that having a baby meant she would have to stop working for quite some time. Struggling financially was not in her plan—ever.

Ronnie Sue worked for an attorney in Newark. She took the train and walked up Raymond Blvd to the office. The Newark riots had happened there about a year earlier. On July 12, 1967, a Black cab driver named John Smith was pulled over and badly beaten by the police, in view of a large public housing project, then was dragged to the Fourth Precinct station house. Protestors grew impatient and violence erupted. Ronnie noted, *you didn't cross the big main street; you stayed on the side of your building. Nothing happened during the day. All unrest happened at night and on weekends.*

Three years later, Stuart and Ronnie relocated to Alexandria, Virginia as he had gotten a job with Best Products, a catalog showroom store, after his seven-year service commitment ended. They bought a condo and had to drive all the way to Baltimore to get kosher meat.

I was born in Alexandria in November 1971. I'm guessing Valentine's Day was a good day for my parents that year. *Being new parents was crazy!* Dad's extended family all came down from New Jersey. Mom loved being a new parent and enjoyed taking me on all sorts of sightseeing tours: the National Gallery, dinosaur exhibits, Lindbergh's airplane and Amelia Earhart's audio story in the Air and Space Museum.

Mom told me a story from that time. She always enjoyed a glass of wine, and one of her Italian neighbors had given her some that was homemade, maybe to calm her nerves from being a new parent. Apparently, homemade Italian wine is a bit more potent than what you'd find in the store. *I found my flip flops in the freezer.* I'm sure she made a great impression on the family. She always was a lightweight and not too discerning; boxed white zinfandel over crushed ice was her drink of choice.

In the spring of 1972, they relocated again as Dad opened a new Best Products jewelry department in Dallas, Texas. *It was a beautiful town. We had a couple of close friends. We lived in a great apartment where I was able to take you swimming every afternoon. There was shade over half the pool.* We stayed for about two years, then my parents bought their first house back east in Richmond, Virginia.

I do remember some things about that house, even though I was a small child when we left it. It was a split level with carpeted stairs going up to the bedrooms on the right. I think I once did a cartwheel down those stairs. I had a beautiful white wood furniture set with a four-post canopy bed. Our next-door neighbors had kids and we were friendly with them. There were rose bushes and honeysuckle in the yard that I remember picking young buds off and peeling the tightly bound rose petals one by one and tasting the sweet honeysuckle nectar. I would play in the back yard and whenever I got hurt, Mom would scoop me up onto her lap, hold the boo-boo and say, in a very gentle, whispery voice, "pain....away...pain...away...."

The feeling of that comfort is emblazoned on my soul; this is one of my earliest memories, sitting on her lap, held in her embrace, whispering in my ear. Mom always had a magical quality about her that was very healing. In her final days, once she slipped out of consciousness, I would snuggle next to her and return the favor, "pain...away...pain...away...." I hope that in her mind, she felt the same comfort she had given me when I was a child.

No matter where they were, my parents adored each other and had fun building a life together. We got a dog in Richmond when I was three, a miniature French poodle that Mom lovingly called "Stacey's Magical Muffin." *She used to lay with her nose on the window by the baby grand piano situated in the corner of the living room waiting for Dad to get home from work.* Muffin was with us for about sixteen years; I had never known life without a dog in my space. I remember learning about loss for the first time when she died. I knew the end was near. I think she had developed doggie breast cancer and she wasn't doing well. I remember sitting with her on the floor in my bedroom, snuggling her, whispering in her ear what a good dog she had always been and how much I loved her. I was afraid to let her go, but I knew that our time together was almost done.

In 1977, Pook and Pookie packed up again and we relocated to New York. Dad had an offer to work for a high-end jeweler in Scarsdale. Dad's salary would triple, and he would be paid mileage to commute from wherever he would settle his family, so the move up north was a no-brainer. For a few months, Dad would make the trek from Richmond to Rockland County, New York, where he scouted out homes as they prepared to sell our house. Their broker in Virginia had pulled some newspaper ads about a town called Clarkstown and on one of his commutes, Dad stopped in a hamlet called New City to get a paper to check out the realty section. He wound up finding a four-bedroom, two-and-a-half bath high ranch on Beaver Court in the Clarkstown Central School District. Apparently, that was what got Mom's attention. When the realtor ads highlighted "Clarkstown schools," it was a winner. Another perk: Mom also liked the *countrified feel* of the suburban area.

Our house was at the base of a bucolic cul-de-sac with a lot of kids in the neighborhood. The next twenty years were spent forming who we were in that house. We had a huge yard to run around in with a pool, and the schools were excellent. There was a neighborhood full of kids and we'd all play outside until it got dark. I remember throwing rocks at bats that would swoop down suddenly, making us squeal and run for cover. I played catch with my dad in the front yard, which I proudly cut on our big red Toro riding mower. My tenth birthday present was a 10-speed bike, which took me a few years to grow into, but I remember taking long rides around the neighborhood as a teenager. From the support and trust from my parents, I grew up feeling autonomous and developed confidence, which was instrumental for my transition into adult life.

Every night, Dad would play music on the baby grand, the same one that was in his house growing up; that piano is now in my home. I'd sing over his shoulder and develop a deep love of music and the arts. So many rites of passage from birthday parties to my bridal shower were celebrated there. At thirteen, I became Bat Mitzvah. Mom recalled it as a *sparkling event*, mostly because she made it so. Before the big day, she threw a family dinner at home to commemorate the event where her sisters and Mollye helped her cook a dinner spread that was to die for. Mom remembered even Grandma Adelaide complemented her saying "Oh, this is such a good party!"

Mom would make the Passover Seder every year (putting her training into practice) and extended the dining room table for guests. One year, we had a major snowstorm in April and my mom had prepared to host twenty-seven family and friends. Even with the blanket of snow cover, the Seder went on.

Dad was a simple eater, pretty much meat and potatoes with the occasional salad or microwaved frozen vegetable.

Despite the legacy of culinary experts in her family, Mom wasn't much of a chef herself during most of the year. However, Passover was her time to shine. Mollye taught her well in that respect; she went all out for the Seder. The spread was pretty much the same annually: brisket, noodle kugel, carrot tzimmes and gefilte fish from a jar were the staples. She also made an array of Pesach desserts; spongy angel food cake was a regular in the rotation, which I loved, but my favorite was always chocolate-covered coconut macaroons from a can.

One of her culinary talents in Jewish cooking was her matzah ball soup, which I loved. She'd make the balls two ways—light and fluffy for some, small and hard as a rock for others (me). To this day, a couple times a year, I try to emulate that talent, and I have passed it on to my older daughter who loves making and eating them. In the year of twenty-seven guests, Mom had made a huge pot that was simmering on the stove. Grandma Adelaide, feeling it necessary to "help," brought cans of soup broth and started pouring them into the pot. The problem was the cans had been damaged and the broth was rancid.

Adelaide had, unintentionally, ruined Mom's masterful matzah ball soup. She'd suggested that maybe they could scoop the balls out and still have them for dinner. (Oy.) Mom was heartbroken as Dad and his friend Michael had to drag the giant pot to the backyard and pour the soup into the creek. Mom lamented, *What's Passover without matzo ball soup?* I think this incident didn't exactly help relations between Mom and Grandma Adelaide.

When we arrived in New City, we joined the local synagogue, and my parents enjoyed belonging to the temple until, as Mom put it, *it went crazy.* Back in Richmond, we belonged to a small conservative synagogue and had made a pledge to the building fund of $2000 over the course of ten years. When we got to New York, they allowed my parents to carry over the remainder of that pledge from Virginia, about $800. However, years later, a new board had come in and nixed the original agreement. Dad didn't like that and made a huge stink (Mom said, *there was a brouhaha*), and we left shortly after my Bat Mitzvah for a calmer, quieter synagogue a little further away from home where Dad re-started the Men's Club and was a part of the Chevra Kadisha, where he helped care for the bodies of synagogue members who had died. My father would daven like a pro, sweetly and piously singing harmonies to all of the prayers as he swayed side to side, back and forth, almost as though it was his job as an assistant Cantor. I can still hear his voice in my head singing specific sections of the prayers and while I fell away from religious practice for myself, I am still able to participate in the singing of many of the songs and contribute harmonies just like my father did whenever I attend a Jewish event in shul. I like to think that wherever he is, he can hear and be proud that he had that lasting impact on me.

Apparently, he had a lasting impact on many people. Mom recalls, *After your daddy died, I remember in the synagogue, Lenny Zimmerman* (our family physician and synagogue board member) *came up to me after the service and said, 'I will always miss your husband's bellowing harmonies during all the prayers.'*

When we lived in Richmond, my parents had found a kosher supermarket in Baltimore, which they were happy to make the commute since it meant they could keep kosher, as promised to Adelaide and Sam. However, in New City, the only place to go was Spring Valley, home to a large community of Orthodox and Hasidic Jews. It seemed to be a perfect fit; they could go to the butcher in Spring Valley about twenty minutes away, and they would be able to maintain the promise to keep a kosher lifestyle. Unfortunately, when Mom stepped foot inside, *the place was gross*. The butcher wore an apron with old, dried blood on it. She was completely horrified and immediately had a conversation with Dad. Mom vowed that she would keep the kitchen "kosher style," but would not buy from the guy in Spring Valley. Dad agreed and had the unfortunate job of telling Adelaide. Apparently, that's when Mom fell out of

Adelaide's good graces. When I was growing up, there was always tension in the family. As a kid, I never knew why, but this break from traditional kosher living certainly explains a lot.

My Dad, as loyal as he was to his parents and family, was utterly devoted to my mom. Occasionally, he would bring sea scallops home for us to eat, even though it went completely against his kosher sensibilities. My parents accepted each other for who they were, even if it meant there would be some challenges to contend with, and they endured a lot of them. Though I do remember lots of loud arguments and serious discussions, there were also lots of hugs, smiles and laughter. He loved spending time with his dream woman, his Pook. For better or worse, they had a real, long-lasting marriage—one I have as a model for my own relationship with my husband. They truly adored each other.

When I asked Mom to talk about him, she paused for a moment, took a breath, and said, *"He was such a good man."* Mom always knew he was a mensch, something Dad always aspired to be.

Our Broken Heart

If there ever comes a day
when we can't be together,
keep me in your heart.
I'll stay there forever.

~ A.A. Milne, *Winnie the Pooh*

In September 1993, right after I graduated from college, Dad had been complaining about feeling like it was hard to breathe—like there was a lump in his throat. Doctors had originally said he had some sort of respiratory ailment, maybe a sinus infection. The problem never resolved itself and he had to look closer into the problem. On my twenty-second birthday, he saw a head and neck surgeon who diagnosed him with thyroid cancer. The doctor scheduled a surgery about a week later for the Wednesday before Thanksgiving. I remember being scared for my dad; like my grandmother, Mollye, the tumor had grown extensively and had wrapped itself around his trachea.

The surgery would be an extremely invasive procedure and there was a strong chance that he would also lose the ability to speak if his voice box had to be removed. For someone whose greatest talents were singing, talking and telling an off-colored joke, this news was a devastating blow. I remember him sitting at the kitchen table as he told me the news. I don't think I took it very well. I was also in the middle of performances for a cabaret show in the city, and I was preoccupied with how I would manage being there for my dad's recovery and fulfilling my duty to the show. Either way, it was happening, so on the morning of the surgery, Mom took him to the hospital.

The procedure took a long time, and Mom recalls, *they kept coming out saying 'he's doing okay, but we haven't gotten clean margins yet.'* The surgery was tricky, and his trachea would become shorter because the tumor was so invasive. When the doctor finally came out and said he got clean margins, he explained what would happen over the next several weeks. Dad's chin was sewn to his chest to facilitate healing and he wouldn't be able to talk for weeks, if not longer. It was going to be a long recovery, but the surgery was successful.

Seeing Dad laying in the hospital bed, chin sewn to chest, intubated and still, it was so opposite to his natural state of being. There was so much fear and hope to process; I had never experienced any kind of family trauma like this. It may have been the first time I felt like I was standing on unstable ground, not knowing how to accept the situation I was in. Nonetheless, he was alive and had a chance for some sort of recovery.

The next day was Thanksgiving. While Mom stayed in the hospital with Dad, I had dinner at Chris' house. His parents, Ivonne and Pete, were so loving and kind, and truly absorbed how shaken I was about my father. They took care of me, as they always had, and for a few hours, helped alleviate the stress of a very difficult situation.

That Friday, we spent the day visiting Dad in the hospital and hanging out with him. The hospital staff apparently had been scrambling all day to keep him alive; the surgery had created so much damage in his airway that they were doing diagnostic testing, x-rays, etc. to monitor him constantly and worked hard to keep an airway open. Dad had always suffered from post-nasal drip due to allergies, and this was allergy season.

I was hanging out in his room, and he started struggling to breathe. Medical staff started rushing in and I was quickly ushered out of the room. Standing behind the closed ICU double door looking through the tiny window, I wondered what the hell was happening. Mom had just returned from dropping Adelaide off at the house. It felt like I was in a black hole, watching people rush in and out of the room for what felt like an eternity.

Dad had formed a mucus plug that wound up blocking his airway. Apparently, when the medical staff ran in, they couldn't clear the plug in time. When the doctor came out to us, we were informed that Dad had died. It was like my soul had been sucked out of me in an instant. I screamed and felt my legs turn to jelly. I don't remember much else other than sitting in a waiting room wondering how life was supposed to move forward. Mom remembered being in absolute, total shock. This was not supposed to be the end of their story. Thyroid cancer was not supposed to take Dad's life.

I remember going into his room where he lay, kissed his cheek, and implored him to go straight to heaven, as if his soul were sticking around while we were still in the room. He was still warm, but uncharacteristically, very still. He was always moving, vibrant, so full of life. Even when he slept, he snored like a buzz saw. It permeated the walls throughout the house.

I couldn't fathom that this would be the last time I'd ever see my father. There was so much left unsaid, so many things we needed time to work out. The tragedy of that circumstance was something I did not want to repeat with my mom at the end of her life.

Eventually, it was time to go home. Chris took me and his dad, Peter, brought Mom home from the hospital. *He was so supportive and caring. Even though I was literally in shock, his voice was very comforting.* Our high school friend, Vinny, had come to the house to analyze Dad's meticulous financial ledger sheets. Mom remembers, *that was the most pressing question on my head then: was I going to be able to support us.* He assured her that we would be fine. Grandma Adelaide was there at the house, confused and a complete mess. She had lost her eldest son. A mother is not supposed to outlive her children.

When I asked Mom if she had the time to mourn, she responded:

> *I had no time. I had to keep going and do what had to be done. I'm not the kind of person to dwell on things that I can't change. That was probably good for me because to me, when a person mourns, they're not really achieving anything; it's more of a 'woe is me.' I never wanted to take time to answer those questions. There is no answer. I was grateful to have things to think about and decisions to make about the welfare of myself and my family. I remember friends coming to the house. It was*

*comforting, but I just wanted people to do their
thing and go home because I just wanted to be
with my family.*

Then the food came in. Casseroles. Fruit baskets. Chopped
liver. Chickens. Whole meals. The dining room table with
the extensions was too small to fit it all. Cheryl, the
organizer, alphabetized everything in the big freezer
downstairs and the spices in the kitchen. She also made
detailed lists of what was there and instructed Mom how to
cross things off the list when she finished them. Michael and
Janet, close friends of my parents, were there consoling
Mom. Michael told Mom that anytime they were coming up
the driveway for a visit, they always heard music playing and
singing. It was one of those things that stuck with him. It
took a while for them to want to go home. As Michael
tearfully talked to Mom, he said to her, "You'll be okay." *He
left me okay financially. Janet just sat and held my hand.
Finally, everyone realized it was time to go home—except
Chris and Vinny.* They could stay. To her, they were family.

Side note: the day that Mom died, I received a phone call
from a tearful Janet. She had called my house and got my
cell number from Chris. I sat on the floor, and we talked and
cried together, and she told me what a special person my
mother was. It was nice to hear her voice—a connection to
the past that I remember fondly. She and Michael came to

the funeral to pay their respects, even though they hadn't seen each other in many years.

With the shiva week done, Mom went right back to work. Despite the dire situation, she always chose to keep herself busy. Ever the pragmatist, she had worked on the playbill for Coupé's Nutcracker while sitting in the hospital as my dad was recovering. I think the distraction kept her from completely breaking down. What's funny is that Mom never let on that she was worried. I know she didn't ever want people to think she was not okay. I knew that she was very sad, for a long time, but she kept pressing onward. With Dad gone, she now had to redefine her life without him.

Running With the Law

You can only become truly accomplished at
something you love.
Don't make money your goal.
Instead pursue the things you love doing and
then do them so well
that people can't take their eyes off of you.

- Maya Angelou

Mom always worked. Coming from a long line of career women, she happily followed suit, only taking a break as a young mom and my dad was secure in his career. Once I was school-age, she went back to work, and I became the classic latch-key kid of the 1980's. I came home from school, got a snack (usually pop tarts or cereal that made the milk chocolatey), and sat on their king-sized bed to watch TV.

In 1977, when the Roths moved to New York, Mom was able to stay home and be a mom. When Dad's job in Scarsdale didn't pan out and he became unemployed for a little while, she went back to work for a local attorney for a couple of years. She didn't like that office much and answered an ad for Richard Licata, a new attorney just starting his own practice. Mom was hired (of course) and helped Rich as a paralegal as he built his practice. He later hired a young associate named Alan Brill, who later became a partner. Mom and Alan shared a birthday and developed a close relationship as friends and confidantes. In total, she worked with Rich and Alan for about ten years. She was an integral part of their law firm until the firm dissolved in 1991. Once again, it was time to find a new job.

Ronnie Sue's job search lasted two days. She was hired by Marvin Stillman for his partner Charles Spiegel, as his legal assistant. It was a match made in heaven. The only caveat was the long trip over the Tappan Zee Bridge to East Tremont Avenue in the Bronx. It was quite a change for her, adding so much commuting time to her workday, but it was a position that fueled her legal spirit. Eventually, ever the early bird, Mom would leave the house around 5 a.m. to avoid the rush hour traffic. That gave her some quiet time in the office to get more work done before the rush came in. It also ensured she'd get good street parking.

She recalled that the biggest challenge of her new position was the eventual dissolution of Stillman and Spiegel. She was invited to sit in with the partners and office administrators to take notes of the different agreements that would constitute the dissolution of the partnership, and the formation of the two new partnerships of Stillman and Stillman, and Spiegel and Barbato. She recalled the meeting lasted more than seven hours and resulted in five separate agreements which had many terms that had to be ironed out. Mom organized the terms of the agreements herself to help them financially ease the process and get them signed in the most financially efficient manner with the least amount of distress. This was quintessential Ronnie Sue, always working to make people's lives better. If her involvement meant a smoother, more streamlined process, it was a job well done.

As she continued her career with the new Spiegel and Barbato partnership, Mom explained how Mr. Spiegel recognized how much knowledge Mom came to the firm with and was insistent that she help grow the firm in a managerial capacity. Hence, her title of "Supervising Paralegal." Nowadays, most paralegals have to earn a specialized degree to get that designation. Mom's title was recognized solely through her expertise and work product.

Mom's major role was to keep the practice running efficiently together with the office manager. She managed personnel, implemented weekly agendas for training of legal assistants and new attorneys with Lucille Barbato, and conducted research and writing for Mr. Spiegel. She made the staff under her tutelage feel included in the process of their legal education and was a conduit for efficiency.

Over the years, Mom developed a close working relationship with Charles and Lucille. She looked out for them and always worked in their best interests. Even in retirement, Mom enjoyed working remotely when she moved to Houston. It was more than a job; she considered it *a privilege to be able to continue one's life's work even at the age of 72. That doesn't happen often.* Mom recalled a text message from the summer of 2020 that Charles sent to her that said, "You've always been my inspiration!" Yes, Mr. Spiegel. She's my inspiration too. Always has been, always will be.

On the night Mom passed, I had a long conversation with Lucille. I think it gave both of us some solace to connect with someone who we knew Mom loved dearly. Like everyone else who was close to Ronnie, she was utterly heartbroken. She had emailed with Ronnie every single day of her retirement and shared how Ronnie's morning messages always rang out "Gooooood Morning!" Mom knew how to make the most of writing in a virtual space.

Lucille told me that she, Charles, and Mom acted as a unit— the three were like one. While they understood that in the last four years Mom's work contributions would be more sporadic while she was in treatment, they still valued her desire and ability to provide service to the success of the firm. Even through Mom's medical downslides, she would wake up at four in the morning, make her way to her desk, and click away at the computer, working on files or organizational projects. Ronnie Sue was devoted to the law, and to Charles and Lucille, and I am grateful to them for giving her the opportunity to spend almost thirty years engaged in the work that she loved so dearly.

*****

A few years after Dad died, Mom decided to go back to school to finish the degree she had started years prior. After working for so many years in the legal field, Ronnie Sue had an aspiration to possibly pursue a law degree. She already knew so much about the profession and was quite adept at writing and editing legal documents, researching and engaging para-professionals, attorneys and judges, all with ease and confidence, so it wasn't a far stretch. It was a passion that maybe, just maybe, it was time to take to the next level.

At almost fifty years old, Mom enrolled in Nyack College's adult education program, a local school with flexible classes, which combined her credits from LSU with life credit term papers. I think the process was a cathartic one for her; she could expound upon her experiences over the previous thirty years and let the words fall onto the page. She knew she had to finish her bachelor's degree in order to move forward with her aspirations, and she decided it was time to go "all in."

Ronnie Sue completed her Bachelor of Science degree in Organizational Management in 1998. She finished in two and a half years, all the while working full-time. Her final thesis was called "How to Better the Management of the Law Firm of Stillman and Spiegel." When Mr. Spiegel read it, *Charles actually cried*. Ronnie knew how to deeply touch people in their soul. The cherry on top... Though Nyack College didn't have an official valedictorian, she was chosen to give the opening remarks for graduation. Her topic was how Helen Keller overcame the most tremendous adversity. Apropos for a woman who had to pick up the pieces of her life after losing her one true love.

After graduation, Mom was free to take her passion for the law a step further. Following some careful soul-searching, she decided she wanted to take a leap of faith and go to law school and had the support of everyone around her.

> *I had a letter of recommendation from Henry Miller. He had a chair on the board at Pace University. We had a trial through Stillman and Spiegel that we referred to him and I worked with him on the trial. He wrote the most glowing recommendation I've ever had the honor to read.*

The biggest obstacle was the Law School Admission Test (LSAT). Now in her early 50s, Mom would be sitting for the law school entrance exam most 20-somethings just out of college have trouble passing. I think about the idea of sitting for a test like that now. The last major exam I took was for my third teaching certificate almost ten years ago. I think about the stress, the preparation, and the brain fog from the regular aging process. As brilliant as she was, I was amazed she would choose to put herself at the foot of a path that would take another four years to complete.

Ultimately, Mom did not follow that path. After taking the LSAT twice and receiving scores that were lower than her school of choice accepted for admission, she decided that law school was out. As much as I respected and supported her decision, there was always a quiet piece of me that was saddened by it. First, I can only imagine the disappointment she must have felt deep down. She would never admit it, but she had her mind so wrapped up in this venture. I think she imagined herself in this new role and really wanted it to come true. Second, and perhaps a more selfish reason, I liked the idea that I might refer to my mom as Ronnie Sue Roth, Esq. After all, she was smarter and more talented than most of the attorneys out there. From all accounts, she also knew how to sweet talk a judge. Her natural southern charm came in quite handy in professional circles.

I always marveled how much respect and adoration she had from her colleagues—even the myriad attorneys she interacted with throughout her career sought her counsel with regularity. I know that in the end, she was completely satisfied with her role in the office. Even though my mind did sometimes wander to what might have been, I have always had a deep sense of pride in all of her professional accomplishments. She was my greatest role model.

Extracurriculars

Determine never to be idle.
No person will have occasion to complain of
the want of time who never loses any.
It is wonderful how much may be done if we
are always doing.

~ Thomas Jefferson

I never remember my mom spending idle time when I was growing up. Even when she was resting, she'd always have a book or something creative in her hands, almost working on autopilot with the television on in the background. She had a ton of creative energy, loved using her brain and really thrived when she was working on making something beautiful.

As a young mother in New City, Dad said she had to learn a "parlor game." I wouldn't think this was exactly how Mom wanted to spend her spare time, but in deference to Dad's suggestion, she read the directions and learned how to play mah-jongg once a week with three other local moms. I have a sense memory of the miniature suitcase of plastic tiles that clicked together as they were spread out on the card table. It was fun and social but didn't rock Ronnie's world and the pastime didn't last for too long. It wasn't exactly the mental stimulation or creative outlet she craved. I remember seeing the case collecting dust up in the coat closet for many years after she abandoned the activity.

Even as a full-time mom with a full-time job, Mom had some energy to spare. She had a lot of interests and as opportunities presented themselves, she took advantage of them. Dad was supportive and encouraging of Mom working; the extra income was helpful since he was sometimes in and out of work, and we were living in an area where the Joneses were expected to be kept up with. His struggle was with her becoming so involved with her other activities. Time was limited and he lamented the time she spent away from the family unit after work and on weekends, but Mom had developed strong connections with the people on the outside. Sometimes it was volunteering, other times side work to help with extra cash. She was a self-professed workaholic and always wanted to keep busy. I guess that was built into the genetic code as well.

When we were younger, Mom had done some work volunteering for the local Democratic Party and attended conventions in New City. She was happy to do her part in local politics until she became disillusioned by the inconsistencies and flip-flopping of the candidates. *It didn't make sense to me.* So, she abandoned politics. Things she determined were worth her effort *had* to make sense. She applied this rule to friendships as well. If she felt that people's actions weren't sensible, she quietly backed away.

Mom had a few very close friendships in her circle. Unlike Mollye, she was not a flittering socialite. Instead, she worked hard and then valued her quiet down time at home. I think you could call her an extroverted introvert. When in public, she knew how to shine; she attracted people easily and was looked upon as a leader. At home, sitting in her bed was her favorite place to be, watching television, reading, knitting, or needlepointing. It was her way of unplugging and resetting herself. This was where conversations could be had; debriefings of the day and problems were hashed out sitting at the foot of her bed. Chris remembers, "I remember our best conversations happening with me standing at her bedside. It was the weirdest thing to me, to be invited into someone's bedroom with that person lying in her bed, to have a conversation one would normally have at a dinner table. But it made me feel like part of the family."

Flower arranging was another activity Mom loved spending her time doing. There was something about the hands-on nature of the work where she would start with an empty container and in a few minutes, a masterpiece would be created. She had such a gift for the creation of beautiful things. Early on, she developed a working relationship with a local florist who made the princess bouquets for Coupé's annual production of The Nutcracker; one of her volunteer duties was to order and pick them up and bring them to the performances.

One day, she went in to pick the bouquets up and the florist hadn't gotten to make them yet. The store was crazy busy, so she offered to make them herself to alleviate his stress. Apparently, she did a great job because he asked if she wanted to learn floral design. He could use the help on the weekends, particularly with events, and she could make a few extra dollars. Excitedly, she agreed and started working on Saturdays. Eventually, he asked her if she knew anyone else who might be interested in working, so she brought me in to train as well. We worked together, side by side, cleaning flowers and making arrangements of all shapes and sizes.

I learned how to make funeral and wedding arrangements, dozens of roses in vases and boxes, big, decorative bows out of rolls of ribbon, English gardens, and Christmas arrangements—all the while spending time with my mom. I loved working with her and watched her like a hawk. I just wanted to acquire even a little bit of the creativity and vision she had for floral design. I was good, but her work was exquisite. Eventually, we took our talents to another local florist, and I worked there for years following high school, only stopping once I started my teaching career.

Mom used her talent to help other friends of hers who owned a store that sold seasonal decorative merchandise. She would work the Christmas season making pine wreaths and garlands. That was the funny thing about Mom; if the activity fueled her passion, she had a seemingly never-ending supply of energy. If someone needed her, she was there, and she not only helped, but she found ways to improve things. She was pretty remarkable in that way.

*****

Mom was particularly drawn to the performing arts. Only once was she a performer herself; her claim to fame was in a community production of *L'il Abner* in 1963 where she took a turn as Stupefyin' Jones. I found an old program and some pictures from the production in the bag of letters at the bottom of her closet. She wore a fancy leotard with a satin cape. She had great legs. That was the extent of her thespian career.

The summer I was going into high school, my parents saw an ad in the local paper announcing auditions for Clarkstown Summer Theater Festival, a local summer drama program for teens. I had done a junior high school production of *Bye Bye Birdie* and started to show some interest in performing. They encouraged me to join CSTF so I would have something to do over the summer before entering high school. I had a great time, and after that first summer experience, I was interested in taking dance classes. Before that, I was always involved in Hebrew school and becoming Bat Mitzvah, but now that the religious commitment was done, I had more free time on my hands. They saw how much I got from the program, especially the social exposure (I was a very shy kid) and they both decided to volunteer to help this organization.

Because of my parents' support, I attended the program every summer through high school graduation and with each production, they wanted to help the program prosper and thrive even more. A nice bit of nostalgia was that my last production with CSTF was *L'il Abner*. I played Appassionata Von Climax. Underage sex symbols aside, my parents saw what an incredible thing youth theatre did for my confidence and was a springboard that launched me into high school theatre, which led me to pursue a theatre degree in college, and ultimately, a career in the performing arts and education. It had given me so much experience and personal growth, and it seemed to fit nicely in my parent's paradigm of what was good for kids.

Mom got involved on the board, through various committees and eventually was voted in as board President for a few years after I graduated. Dad offered his organizational and fundraising talents to get ad sales for the playbill, raising thousands of dollars in just a few short weeks. He would take groups of kids to strip malls and teach them how to walk into stores, give a pitch to get them to solicit advertising, and walk out with a check.

After that first summer, my parents enrolled me in a tap and jazz classes at Coupé Theatre Studio, owned by former Broadway dancer Diane Coupé Frankel. Every year, we would participate in an annual recital called "Demo" and my mom was recruited to help manage the dancers backstage, so the flow of the performance ran smoothly. Mom loved to tell the "Bag Lady Story"...

> *At your first end-of-year recital, I was working backstage, helping move groups of kids from the dressing areas to the stage. A woman, holding bags of costumes, came down the hallway and stopped me to ask if I was Stacey Roth's mother. Curious and intrigued, I said yes. Then the bag lady introduced herself as Diane Frankel, the owner of the studio, who*

had apparently taken some interest in you. Diane insisted that you take more classes next year and that she would offer you a scholarship for as many classes as you wanted to take.

The bag-lady story was what got her hooked on Coupé. As the years passed, she grew more active in the studio, helping Diane produce the shows and eventually assisted as she was forming the Rockland Youth Dance Ensemble (RYDE), which was a student dance company that gave more serious dance students the opportunity to train harder and shine brighter. *With Coupé, I was making an effective change that I couldn't give up. I was a little selfish; I knew that Daddy was upset by it, but I just couldn't give it up...like somebody on drugs.*

That concept of being "effective" is something that I have absorbed into my life's philosophy, and it is in the back of my mind with everything I do. Wherever I spend my energy, I just want to know the effort was fruitful in some way. If I can help even one person with my intervention, the energy spent is well-worth it. That's what Mom was all about— helping people become better versions of themselves. And so, I follow her lead.

RYDE became a major force in Mom's world. She helped write the mission statement, get the organization up and running and served on the board as President and eventually Chairman of the Board for many years. *I watched a lot of student advancement. I enjoyed it but didn't understand the artistry behind the work.* Of course, that didn't matter. She was the production support for the artistic staff to do what they do best—help kids achieve and excel in the performing arts.

When it was time to move to Houston, Ronnie stepped down from her role as Chairman of the Board. They celebrated her service, gifting her with a beautiful pewter engraved platter. She looked at that plate every single day in Houston, as it sat on her dressing room table. It now rests in my home, serving as a reminder of her dedication to service, and of her indelible part in my own development in the arts.

Ronnie loved every minute of her passion projects; seeing kids achieve fed her soul. I took it for granted then, but as she modeled her skills, talents, and work ethic, I learned how much more I was capable of accomplishing. I think that is why I have been so successful working with adolescents. I look at teenagers and see their potential; the possibilities for success are infinite. Of course, the work is in giving them the skills and confidence to explore those possibilities. This is something Ronnie Sue knew, and she was the archetype of her special blend of passion, energy, drive, and belief that enabled me to identify the capabilities of young people and teach them how to follow through on their potential.

Sister of the Soul

*There are friends,
there is family,
and then there are friends
that become family.*

~ unknown

Mom made friends wherever she went. Some relationships lasted for years, others came and gracefully went. She never made a fuss or argued with people. She recognized that you can disagree and still be kind. When you are kind, *it comes back to you tenfold*. But when her personal philosophies clashed with someone else, and things were looking ugly, she realized it was just time to move on.

Mom would never go out of her way to harm someone with words, as much as she might disagree. She would present her ideas, then pull back. She understood that she may have felt strongly about something in a discussion, but the person you're talking to also has their strong feelings based on their experience and ideas. It wasn't about winning; the discussion was always more important to her. That's why she got along so well with Chris. Sometimes they were on opposite ends of a dynamic discussion, but they both thrived on presenting arguments, facts, and challenging each other to make things make sense. They were very much aligned in that wisdom, and I always marveled how they could go at it for hours and in the end, move on to other topics.

Though Mom made and kept many friends in her life, there were two women who she would consider "soul sisters to the end." These were the women with whom she could talk for hours—about philosophy, family, work and projects; she could share herself honestly and completely with them. They could go weeks without talking and then pick up as though no time had passed.

*****

Mom met Lona through RYDE. Lona was a young Coupé parent who had sent her resume in for a production position with the studio. Mom was so impressed with her resume and personal intention. She called Diane (Remember the bag lady? They became good friends.) and said that Lona was a person for the studio. They had lunch together to discuss what Lona had to offer Coupé and RYDE. Of course, if my mom was going to bat for you, you were as good as in.

Lona was hired by both organizations. By working together through every Nutcracker and Demo, they got closer. Ronnie became part of the family. Mom used her crafting skills to help Lona with her kids' Bar Mitzvah decorations, to make a shadowbox after her son Rory's wedding and a beaded envelope handbag for her daughter Rachel's wedding. Mom fell in love with Lona's family early on, and they fell right back in love with her. Ronnie recalls:

> *She made everything so effortless. She's a brilliant woman and I'm so connected to her in a way; it started with the binding of two hearts, and it just never strayed from that. I may not talk to her every day or week, but she'll always reach out. I've enjoyed her friendship— very close to a sisterhood. Neither of us ask for anything from each other. We just give.*

Mom used to go to Lona and her husband Kip's every January 1st for a New Year's welcome party. When Mom moved down south, Lona started inviting me. At first, I thought it was in part to get some semblance of a "Ronnie fix." Lona insists it's to get her "Stacey fix." I'll take that. Over the last few years, I have gotten closer to Lona, and we have enjoyed sharing a perspective of Ronnie through each other's eyes. It is comforting to be close to someone who knew her so well.

*****

Sheila is one of Mom's oldest friends from when she and Dad got engaged. Sheila had dated Dad back in his Jersey Shore days. Actually, she had dated both Dad and Zel at the same time. Zel was going to Temple University for dentistry and Dad was doing his time in the Air Force Reserves. The three of them used to go to the Jersey Shore together with a group of friends from North Jersey. These were the days when Dad was still playing gigs with his event band. I suppose at some point, Sheila had to decide between the two men; she eventually picked Zel.

Of course, Dad didn't give up easily. On the day of Sheila and Zel's wedding in 1966, Stuart, ever the rebel, goes to the bridal suite dressed like a waiter. He asked Sheila, "Are you sure you want to marry Zel? Last chance!" Of course, she married Zel. Sometime later, they had Dad over for dinner— burnt chicken, which apparently was a style that Zel loved. Dad, taking one look at the bird said, "You married the right one!"

Through the years, as both couples had their children, we would visit Sheila and Zel in Boston regularly. We'd stay at the house and hang out on their boat; Zel was an avid sailor and was proud to take us sailing in the harbor. The kids would play together, and I always grew up calling them aunt and uncle. I was well into adulthood when I learned that we weren't really related by blood...only by history. *It was a torrid love affair amongst four people. It was a wonderful evolution of a friendship.*

After the husbands passed, Ronnie and Sheila's sisterhood lived on. One thing Mom learned from Mollye was that if you stop learning from a friend, then your relationship has run its course. About her friendship with Sheila:

> *It's effortless. It's just plain fun. There isn't a day that passes that she doesn't come up with some outstanding idea. She's full of soul and spunk; I love her to pieces. She lifts my day like no other. Sheila and I...we'll always be connected.*

Deep in the Heart of Texas

Maybe I don't know that much.
But I know this much is true.
I was blessed because I was loved by you.

~ Diane Warren, *Because You Loved Me*

In 2014, Mom moved to Houston, Texas. Ronnie had been missing her sisters and the "southern way" after living in Yankee territory for forty years. The house on Beaver Court was sold and a new adventure had begun. I missed her terribly, and when she told me that Mr. Spiegel had asked her to come back to New York in 2016 for a few months to help train some new people, she asked if she could stay with me. Needless to say, I was elated. I got her room ready right away and prepared to enjoy some good Mom-time.

The plan was for her to stay with us September through November, then she'd return to Houston in time for Thanksgiving. We had a great time hosting Mom. We celebrated her birthday with a cake that said, "Happy

Birthday, Glitza!" My girls were so happy to see their Nanny in their house and we truly enjoyed each other's company every single day. We'd come home from work and school, have dinner together, and hang out. There were never conflicts or stress; it was always easy and fun. I've always been fortunate that my husband adored his mother-in-law, and he welcomed the chance to have her close to us.

Chris and I had been planning our 20th wedding anniversary party at the end of November—a big hullabaloo with friends and family. Mom would attend the party and return home to Texas. She was gorgeous that night...radiant really. She had reunited with her soul sister, Lona, and watched her family celebrate a milestone. As joyous an occasion as it was, it was tinged with underlying trepidation.

The week before the party, Chris, the girls, and I were at a restaurant celebrating Sophie's birthday with some of her friends. Earlier that week, Mom had noticed that her abdomen had been swelling significantly. Feeling it was not normal, she took herself to the hospital that afternoon. I met up with her later that evening at the hospital. The doctors tapped her abdomen and they had pulled out five liters of fluid. Her bloodwork showed an elevated CA-125 result—a marker for cancer. The fluid was a result of ascites, an accumulation of fluid in the abdominal cavity, due to the presence of peritoneal cancer. A pitched battle with a horrible disease had begun.

After the party, Mom packed up and headed back to Houston, where she would begin her treatment plan. She started the journey at MD Anderson, the hospital where both her mother and I were treated for our thyroid cancers. My grandmother had lived for many years following her surgical and medical treatments. My story, thankfully, has had a "happy ending" since 1996. It was my mom who led the way for my medical care, acting with adept precision to get me the treatment I needed.

*****

My original treatment was in New York's St Luke's Roosevelt Hospital, where my first surgery was deemed successful by the surgeon, but ultimately, my endocrinologist did not agree. There was apparently a difference of opinion of what "clean margins" meant, and Mom in her infinite wisdom was not going to play around with my health. She had lost her husband to thyroid cancer gone awry and saw what her own mother was going through, and she immediately contacted my grandmother's team in Houston. The second procedure was scheduled, and we took a trip down south to my Aunt Cheryl's house where I would recover post-surgery.

To put that experience into perspective: Ronnie Sue had lost her husband less than three years before my diagnosis. As we healed from that loss, I started commuting with her into the city to start my fledgling career as a singer and actress. Musical theatre was my life. I spent my days auditioning and taking classes and took regional theatre contracts as they came. I eventually started directing and choreographing local school shows as a side gig and got a foothold in a school where I had the opportunity to develop a new career. I had also recently gotten engaged, and we were planning my wedding later that year.

From Mom's viewpoint, there was so much at stake, for both of us. She was not about to sit back and see my life implode— not as long as she had the power to act. Mom was all about action...what she could do to make the best outcome happen. Ronnie Sue knew how to pool her resources and make things happen. Once again, looking back on the life I am fortunate to lead, I owe it to her.

*****

Upon her return to Houston after her New York visit, she started off with great confidence in her medical team. MD Anderson is known as the #1 cancer hospital in the world; my grandmother lived for thirty years after her initial diagnosis. Mom's team scheduled an exploratory surgery to see what the cancer actually looked like and intended to debulk and remove as much cancer as possible.

Peritoneal cancer is unlike most other forms. It is a widespread form that "seeds" itself all throughout the gut. Removing it is not like cutting out a tumor, sewing you up and blasting with chemo or radiation. The procedure is quite invasive and often dangerous. Unfortunately, it didn't go as well as they had hoped. During the surgery, while the doctor was trying to remove as much cancer as she could see, Mom's bowel was accidentally perforated. This resulted in a necessary emergency ileostomy.

Basically, to fix the mistake, they shortened her small intestine above the damage and set up an external bag to collect the waste product. Think colostomy bag, but higher up. It was a horrifying wrench in the works that was not supposed to be a part of the plan, but in true Ronnie Sue fashion, she eventually came to accept the situation. Like Mollye's inability to talk, Ronnie would learn to manage the bag. She trusted implicitly that her doctor had her best interests in mind and continued treatment there.

The next three months were all about getting used to a new life paradigm—living with a bag. She also endured regular aggressive chemotherapy treatments. Between the effects of chemo and the lack of nutrition—the placement of the ileostomy was so high on her intestinal tract that the food she ate didn't get absorbed into her system—Mom declined quickly. Whatever she ate basically came right back out, hardly digested. She became dehydrated very easily and had to have regular TPN (liquid nutrition through an IV). saline infusions and semi-regular hospital stays. I got to know the halls and couch-beds of the hospital very well. Some trips I'd fly in, go straight to the hospital and stay there until it was time to fly back. As much as I hated the idea that she was hospitalized, I was so grateful I had the ability to do the drop-and-run. All I ever wanted was to be by her side and to help her heal.

Mom sort of got used to the bag concept and eventually ventured out into the world with it. She even made a New York trip to see us. It was dicey because time was always of the essence with that damn bag. If you didn't empty it in a timely manner, you had a major problem on your hands. It was literally stuck on to her skin with putty and tape. If it got wet, or leaked, it was a disaster. She handled it all with as much grace as she could muster. In New York, we even managed to see a Broadway show while she was visiting. She had an emergency covert system to empty the bag mid-act that involved zipper bags and paper towels if she needed to, and she chose to be brave, despite the naturally heightened anxiety that developed because of all of her medical trauma.

Thankfully, she always had good support around her, no matter where she was.

For months, we had always held out hope that there was some light at the end of the tunnel as the doctor talked about "putting her back together." Getting rid of the bag was a goal that would signal a major milestone in her recovery. Mom was hopeful that enduring the debilitating chemo treatments to minimize the cancer would put her in a better place for the reattachment surgery; she would do whatever it took to get there.

That March, after four months of living with the bag, the doctors scheduled her for the surgery. It was the one thing Mom was counting on to be able to return to some semblance of normal. Unfortunately, the day before the procedure, she got the most disappointing news. The surgeon was pulling the plug, saying that Mom's was too risky a case. And that was it.

Mom continued to lose weight—about eighty pounds in eight months. Over the course of her time at MD Anderson, she had grown wary of her doctors' decisions and went to get a second opinion. She reached out to Dr. Christine Lee, a highly-regarded gynecological oncologist at Memorial Hermann The Woodlands Medical Center in Shenandoah, Texas. At the consultation, Mom reported that Dr. Lee's opinion was that if she did not have the reattachment surgery, she would die of malnutrition. That was a swift kick in the head. Her only options were either starvation or risky surgery.

It didn't take too long to decide to trust Dr. Lee's opinion. Her reputation preceded her; the message was that if anyone could save Mom's life, Dr. Lee could. Ronnie Sue had a renewed faith in the recovery process; maybe she'd get a last-minute extension with some better quality of life. The surgery was scheduled in late September 2017.

Dr. Lee and her team did another debulking (removal of visible cancer) and successfully managed to reattach the separated bowel and get it working again. The recovery was very rough, but in the end, Mom was put back together. Stella the Stoma (as she not-so-lovingly called it) was no more; the bag was gone. Mom now had a chance of survival past the new year.

*****

Mom recovered so well that in May 2018, Dr. Lee gave her the green light for she and I to take a little mini-vacation to Cancun, Mexico where we celebrated the wedding of Dana and Stephen, colleagues from Spiegel and Barbato. Dana was Lucille's niece—a smart, adorable, sweet young woman who had worked for the practice. Stephen was a young associate. When Mom was still in New York, she took a vested interest in the two of them and played "Yente the office Matchmaker." The relationship blossomed, and they decided to get married. Ronnie was invited and took me as her plus one.

The ceremony was a fantastic destination wedding—the first I had ever attended. We danced, drank, and partied it up; seeing Mom's huge smile while grooving on the dance floor was glorious. We spent three splendid days together sunning, drinking, and eating ourselves across the resort. It was a magical adventure that gave us the chance to have an intensely fun mother-daughter holiday together. We realized then that we needed to travel together more often.

A side note to further illustrate the impact that Ronnie had on the people she loved: In January of 2020, during one of my visits to Houston, a text came in from Lucille, "Dana and Stephen need to talk to you." They knew Mom was having a hard time, but they had some good news for her. When they called Mom, they revealed that they were pregnant with their first child, a boy, and they would name him Alexander Ronnie, in honor of her. Let's just say, Mom was a puddle on the floor. That's how important she was to the people who were close to her. Alexander was born a few weeks before Ronnie Sue left this earth. I follow Dana's social media posts and see the progress of her beautiful boy. Every time I see her post something, I see Mom's name and smile.

After our successful trip to Mexico, we wanted to try to capitalize on Mom's temporarily improved health. We knew we weren't totally out of the woods, and we had learned from one of her doctor visits that spring that she would need to go through another round of chemo late that summer...the cancer had grown back. We decided to take another holiday in July 2019 in Naples, Florida. We spent four days playing tourists...walking the main shopping drive, laying on the beach and eating at different restaurants. One of our favorites was The Claw Bar in our hotel. They had a seafood tower that was to die for. We sat cozily in a booth and chowed down. Taking a note from Mollye, we were always planning what our next meal would be, often while we were in the middle of a meal.

One of the things we really liked to do was take long walks, usually from the hotel to the main drag and back. Nothing was more than a mile away, and Ronnie Sue had surprising energy, even in the heat, so we took it slow and enjoyed the time together. It was nice to walk off a meal, passing palm trees and the beautiful pastel architecture of Naples. We especially enjoyed our ice cream dessert treats, which were usually separate trips from the regular meals we ate. The change of pace and space was comforting, especially to take it all in with Mom at my side. I'd offer my elbow, she took it, and we'd stroll together.

I remember one morning we decided to go to the beach. We grabbed some pool towels and took the hotel shuttle and settled ourselves on an empty patch of sand. Mom laid there like a lady in leisure, glam sunglasses shading her eyes with a black bejeweled cowboy hat sitting on her chest, big smile on her face. For a moment in time, everything was okay. She was happy, not struggling with an imminent medical issue and peaceful. For that moment, I was able to take a deep breath and just enjoy being with her. I didn't want it to end, but alas, the afternoon sun was rising, and it was starting to get uncomfortably hot.

We decided to call the shuttle to head back to the hotel. Unfortunately, they reported that there would be a significant delay with the pickup. Mom and I decided what the heck...we'll walk. It was probably ninety degrees. We didn't have water. The trek was about a mile through mostly residential streets. All the while I kept wondering if I was crazy or stupid (both?) for making my seventy-one-year-old mother, who had gone through the ringer with her health in the last two years, walk in the heat, in flip flops. But Penner genetics are tough. We walked slowly and carefully, and we made it. Thankfully, she showed no signs of distress and after some rest and hydration back at the hotel, we were ready for our next meal. We didn't do much else that day (except eat and drink), but it was quite a memory made. I was so proud of her; I think she was proud of herself too.

*****

The news of the return of Mom's cancer was a tough blow, but she was ready to put up a new fight once again. It was time to start another round of chemotherapy. She bravely chugged along, keeping a complex drug cocktail schedule to stay as comfortable as possible through each chemo infusion every three weeks. Whenever I came in for a visit, I'd take a turn setting up her weekly pill regimen. I remember how that exercise alone was maddening to see all of the things she had to take—supplements, hormones, steroids, pain management. And depending on her status, the cocktail changed dramatically. I can imagine how it drove her crazy trying to keep track of everything.

I made a couple of trips back and forth to help when I could. I also realized that a future New York trip for Ronnie Sue was unlikely at this point. The extended chemo was sapping her of her energy and travel was out of the question. Fearing that the worst might be more imminent than I wanted to admit, I started to think about my girls. They needed to see their Nanny one more time. They had both been struggling with school-related stress and anxiety and knowing their grandmother's health was often on the precipice didn't help.

That December, the day after Christmas, I brought them down to see Mom; I think there was a tacit understanding that it would likely be the last time they would see her in person, and it was a chance I didn't want to miss. Mom and I took the girls to our favorite food places; she told her stories to the girls and gave them trinkets and crystal figurines from her curio cabinets. We lit Hanukkah candles in the menorahs I had packed, and I got to spend time in my favorite spot—sleeping next to her and holding her hand. It was just the trip we needed to make together.

Mom continued treatments into the spring, and I had made three more trips in January and February to help with getting her to chemotherapy and caring for her. Even though it wasn't the kind of "fun" trip I wanted to take, I was happy to be there for her.

To make things even more challenging, the COVID-19 pandemic hit in March of 2020. Scheduling chemo infusions became very tricky since the nation was in a lockdown and medical treatments became restricted to "patient only" conditions. The chemo had also ravaged her system by this point, and she was starting to get nasty side effects that were much harder to manage. One condition in particular that she developed was pleurodesis, where fluid had built up around one of her lungs, basically compressing it and making it very difficult to breathe. A drain had to be installed in her side to be able to relieve the pressure every few days. It was a trying time, but as many challenges that were thrown her way, Ronnie Sue persisted and learned how to deal with each frustrating and sometimes frightening setback. It seemed her focus was on survival, on pressing through, and doing what needed to be done to have another day.

Her in-person appointments had shifted to remote video meetings. It was in one of those video appointments that Dr. Lee delivered the news that we didn't ever want to hear; she was just about out of treatment options. Her CAT scan showed that the Taxol treatment option was no longer doing much to suppress the cancer. She suggested Mom try one more treatment, this time with Carboplatin, which the doctors had used way back in the beginning at MD Anderson, and if memory serves, Mom didn't respond well to it. Despite that, she decided to go through with the treatment, hopeful that it might push the cancer back in one forceful dose, but in the two weeks that followed, Mom's condition declined significantly. Eventually, fluid started accumulating around both lungs.

Some hard decisions had to be made in late August. Mom needed regular nurse care and was having great difficulty moving around on her own—probably the harshest reality for someone who was eternally strong, independent, and so full of life. It was time for hospice care. I had planned and canceled two trips that summer because New York State had instituted an automatic self-quarantine for anyone who traveled into New York from a high-COVID state. Texas was one of those states. After talking to Mom on the Monday and Wednesday of that tough week, I decided it was time. I had to see her, be with her, and hold her hand.

I flew down to Houston once more (COVID quarantine be damned) to see Mom. When I showed up at her bedroom door, she did a double take. She weakly asked, *are you really here? "Yes Mom, I'm here."* It was so hard to see her back in that state. I had seen it many times before, usually post-surgery or during a drop-and-run hospital stay. It was something she would never want anyone else to see; she didn't ever want people to think about her in that way. Honestly, I can't blame her. I wouldn't either. I hugged her gently and climbed into bed next to her.

*****

Acceptance of the end-of-life phase is so antithetical to how we live our lives. We spend so much time shoving death into the far future, putting our energy into the process of living, that to consider death as a present inevitability seems...wrong. All Mom ever wanted to do was to live life to the fullest and she took every opportunity to do that. Now, options to fight were exhausted; it was time to prepare for closing out things as gently and appropriately as possible. Mom wanted to be a part of that process.

The next morning was about organizing her "stuff"...all of the things she had collected and made her happy to have in her space...the tchotchkes, the pictures, the things she loved and surrounded herself with over the course of a lifetime. It quickly became clear that this was the time to pack up the things I wanted to take home with me. The whole process was both surreal and with her blessing. She was part of the process, making sure the things that were important to her, or valuable in some way, were going to be with the people she loved most.

I was both disturbed and thankful to be able to have those in-the-moment interactions in the decision-making process. I bubble-wrapped her framed needlepoints and boxed up the pictures, books and trinkets from her closet and curio cabinets. They were the things she touched, created, and loved over the course of her lifetime. The whole time, I would look at her as she slept, thinking how amazed I was at the sense of acceptance she had come to about "what will be will be." She led a good life and seemed content with whatever would happen next. I asked her to reflect on her cancer diagnosis...

> *It's never really brought me down—no 'why me?' This is where the spiritual piece comes in. I don't like that feeling of being sorry for oneself. I've had a really good time in my life. I want to keep going on that path until it doesn't [happen anymore]. To spend time angry, remorseful, negative...it robs every day that I have to enjoy. When it's time, it's time. I had a really good time in my life. I was lucky to have a husband that I could have spent the rest of my life with had it gone differently. I feel very lucky that my life went the way it did. My children, my grandchildren...I absolutely believe in heaven. You can't destroy matter; I resort to the scientific to prove my theory.*

The last few days of decline were especially tough. One morning, the hospice nurse came to do a checkup and as she was leaving, she pulled me aside. Her message was that it was time to tell Mom everything I wanted to say to her, say goodbye, and give her permission to let go. The rest of that morning was so difficult. Everyone had the chance to say what we needed to say. We would laugh, be quiet for a while, cry, and repeat. I would hold her, and like she did when I was a child, I whispered in her ear,

"Pain...away...pain...away." I quietly sang to her as she slept, including the song we danced to at my wedding, "Because You Loved Me." They were the perfect sentiments for me to express to her.

Going quickly was not an option. Ronnie Sue would wake for a while, sometimes with a little burst of energy, then quietly fall back asleep. While she still could, she put a little extra effort when her loved ones spoke to her. This was something the hospice nurse said was typical of people near death. They will sacrifice an enormous amount of energy to show how much they loved the people who need it the most.

As I interviewed Mom for this book, I asked her to talk about Dr. Lee. She had a deep love and gratitude to her for having the courage to take on her complex case. Understanding that their doctor-patient relationship was coming to an end, this is what Mom had to say:

> *I'm going to miss her and her positive attitude. We're going to keep going until we've tried everything. I respect her tremendously. She saved my life. She gave me three more years than I had, and she did it without hesitation. I know that doctors don't like to operate where*

other doctors have operated and messed up. I
can never thank her enough.

This was Ronnie—always operating out of love and
gratitude. I had the opportunity to read Dr. Lee Mom's
thoughts on a video call near the end. Dr. Lee told her she
loved her, she was with her, and she cried softly. It just
shows you how much Ronnie Sue lovingly burrowed into
people's hearts. I am so grateful to Dr. Lee and the team at
Memorial Hermann for being straight with us, caring for
Mom with love and compassion, and knowing when the end
of the road was near.

I am also eternally grateful to three particular home health
nurses: Anna, Jessica, and Lucy. These amazing women
loved and cared for Mom as though she were their own
family. They all looked out for her, particularly when things
were going very wrong. For their devotion to their "VIP
patient," and their professional guidance along the way, I
give my thanks, and I will always remember the passionate
way they treated her like she was one of their own.

*****

Sometime in the middle of the night, I looked around her
room at her empty curio cabinets and mostly bare walls. The
ones that just days before were brimming with her stuff. I
saw her sleeping, breathing shallowly, not able to rouse

easily. Just days before she was eagerly dictating her story to me in between long naps. Now, she had slipped into a coma. I'd never seen anyone in a coma, and I was now seeing it up close and personal. We were just waiting for her body to finally give in to the inevitable. The night before, I had occasionally put the pulse oximeter on her finger, and it registered at 74. It's supposed to be over 95. Thursday night, it didn't register at all. I checked it on my finger and the numbers popped up immediately. Yep, the thing worked.

I looked at her, wondering when it would happen. Tonight? Tomorrow? Next week? I wondered what it will be like without Mom to call or send an emoji to, only to get sent lots of faces with hearts in the eyes and exuberant messages written in all caps. I wondered how I'd feel back at home when I opened the boxes of her stuff and picture frames filled with our faces and the framed needlepoints that adorned the walls in her home for years. I wore her bracelets and rings and when I glanced at them, I saw her hands and wrists and fingernails at the end of my arms—the same hands I would hold and run my fingers over the smooth, marshmallow painted fingernails ever since I was a kid. The same ones that held me when I was sad and clapped for me when I did something well. How do you let go of someone who literally created you, who made you the person you are today?

I guess you don't. Just like I never really let go of my dad when he passed so many years ago. The only difference now was that I could hold onto the belief that when it does happen, they will finally see each other again. They will hug and kiss and call each other Pookie. They will pick up where they left off and be together for eternity. Morty and Mollye will hug their little girl. And we will get another angel looking out for us in the great somewhere.

Everyone Loved Ronnie Sue

Everything was beautiful
Every hour spent together
Lives within my heart
When she loved me

~ Randy Newman, *When She Loved Me*

On September 4, 2020, at 2:20 pm, Mom finally found peace. The shallow breathing would end. She could stop fighting and rest. This was the day when my heart was once again broken into a million pieces. I knew I would be sad but there is a level of emptiness that I cannot describe. After days of labored breathing as her physical body was breaking down, she had a moment of pause, a final exhale, then stillness. The struggle was over. She could be free to dance with Daddy in the clouds and explore the great unknown. It was time she return the extra dose of stardust she was made of to the universe. Maybe now the world could shine a little brighter.

As I started my grieving process, which I knew would likely be long and difficult, I spoke to the people who loved Ronnie over the years, many of whom I have known through her for a long time. Maybe they had connected with Ronnie last week, some maybe not for years, but the fact remained...they were devastated to hear of her passing. To everyone (and I mean *everyone*) she knew, she was a light, a source of love and fierce devotion. After she passed, and I posted the news on Facebook, the messages of love and condolences immediately started pouring in. People whom I haven't heard from for years came out of the woodwork to pay their respects.

The night that she passed, I stayed at my aunt's house; sleeping in Mom's bed was no longer an option. I hugged Jake, her beloved beagle, who was truly sad and confused, and thanked him for loving her. She called him her therapy dog. As I sobbed, he leaned his head into my chest, and we hugged on the floor next to her bed for a long time. We had spent many days and nights, the three of us, sharing space in Mom's bed. He'd lay in between us, then at her feet, then at my feet. With every nurse visit, Jake was right in the middle of things. Sometimes he'd step on Ronnie Sue, making her wince, but he needed to make himself known and check out whoever was treating her. He was also an attention hound and wanted to make sure he'd get his dose of love and pets too. Dogs were always an important part of Mom's life (dog hair be damned) and they all gave her love, comfort, and solace. They got her through some of the most difficult transitions in her life, including my dad's passing and her battle with cancer.

With three glasses of wine and a small pizza consumed, I spent the evening ensconced in a dark, quiet room talking to some of Mom's closest friends. It was pretty much the same conversation over and over: How magical Ronnie was, how connected she was to them, how much she changed their lives for the better. Repeatedly. As I talked, the tears flowed, the laughter crept in, and I felt even more connected to her. I heard my mom's laugh through my own. I looked at my hands and saw hers. I heard, "God, you sound like Ronnie!" I take comfort in that—being the bridge to her in some physical way for the outside world who loved her. I am my mother's daughter. She is, and always will be, in me. Even as event memories fade, I will always be connected to her, and I can have a moment with her, just by looking at my hands.

*****

I asked some of the people closest to her to write their thoughts in tribute to Ronnie Sue.

Aunt Judy, Mom's youngest sister, on Ronnie Sue's impact:

My Beloved Nonnie Nue,

You were my mother when ours was otherwise physically or emotionally occupied. You were my role model as I watched you grow and establish your place in the world. You pioneered the way for me to succeed in your image: you in law, me in medicine.

You raised your girls to be leaders in their fields: educators and role models, wives and mothers, contributors to their communities and beyond. You showed them the way to make a difference in the world by example, supporting them and applauding them as they did just that. You gave your grandchildren, nieces, nephews and more the matrix to know unwavering love, without bounds, and fostered each of them to grow to their highest potentials. You imprinted yourself on all who had the great good fortune to know you so they could experience what true, unbridled love and acceptance looked and felt like.

You hid your brilliance of mind, character, and personality behind a silly persona so as not to overwhelm others or dissuade their engagement. You exuded a constant love and support to those in your circle and mentored those who surrounded your orbit so they, too, may succeed. You, my dearest sister, were the

embodiment of extraordinary. The likes of you
are rare and so very precious and we, your
family, are beyond blessed to have been
warmed by the brilliance of your heart.

Rest, my beloved Nonnie Nue, and know the
huge impact you have had on the people who
knew and loved you and all of those they
touched in return. That impact is indelible and
precious beyond words. Most of all, know that
you were loved beyond measure and will
always remain in the hearts and memories of
those fortunate enough to have been blessed
with your mentorship, your friendship, your
love.

At the end of this message, Aunt Judy noted that she now
had a new guiding principle to help she and her daughter
make a decision when faced with a crossroads in life:
"WWNND." (What Would Nonnie Nue Do?) I think that's
pretty brilliant.

*****

Ronnie's home health nurse, Jessica, who developed an
unbreakable bond with her, was the linchpin in Mom's care
in the last eight months of her life. She looked out for Ronnie
as though she were her own, in her own no-nonsense, Texas-

woman kind of way. Jessica is kind, loving, brilliant and fought with her to the very end.

Jessica, on Ronnie Sue, the nurturer:

> *I first started seeing her in January 2020. I remember when she was assigned to me, I was shocked by her diagnosis compared to her functional condition. After getting to know her, I learned that was "the Ronnie way." She could be feeling so bad but made sure to let me know she was happy to see me, and I was doing a good job. In the beginning she was fragile, and I was always on high alert. I've never seen anyone bounce back the way she did. We adjusted the standard draining process to accommodate her needs, including a way to have a sterile field with Jake (her beloved beagle) still present and constantly critiqued the process to where she was waking throughout the day and taking care of herself independently. I was so impressed with her progress; I had a hard time convincing other nurses of how fragile she had been.*
>
> *We became friends and I started to share details about my husband's injuries. I didn't understand so many legal mistakes had been made and she guided me through the process of making the responsible party admit fault.*

When he would have surgery, she would check on us although she was dealing with her own medical problems. She was always more concerned with how I was than how she was feeling. She told me her experiences of being a spouse/caregiver and encouraged me to be the wife and aide he needed. My marriage would have suffered if she wouldn't have been there for me and taught me to let go of the little things.

Nothing ever broke her spirits, and she was always so positive. When there was a critical problem with the drain in the beginning... Mrs. Roth just got to tapping on her phone, emailing her coworkers and health team all the while calm and composed. She reminded us, everything was okay and took the situation to a much calmer place. So many times, I would have to ask [her caretaker] how she was doing because she never let it show when she was struggling.

I made her my last stop of the day so we could chat, and I wouldn't be rushed. My family expected I would be home late Mondays, Wednesdays, and Fridays because chances were, we would get wrapped up and lose track of time.

One visit I was stressed with life, and she put her arm around me and hugged me so tight all my stress floated away. I ugly cried to the point there was nothing left. I can't tell you what triggered it but when the hug ended, I noticed she was crying too. I apologized and she simply stated, "We all need that sometimes." She reminded me it is okay to be vulnerable sometimes and even the strongest women need a moment. She never met my kids, but she knew all the stories and every visit we picked up right where we left off before. She gave me parenting advice for my strong-willed daughter and taught me to keep calm with my preteen son trying to find his way in this world.

Mrs. Roth taught me so much and I am sure there are more memories I will send over time as they come up. I am a better person for knowing her and an even stronger nurse through caring for her. She became my best friend. She knew every detail of my life and everyone by name who was close to me. She taught me to work hard but take time for the little things. She would remind me periodically I was put in nursing for a reason, and I know now it was to meet her. I have never connected

with a patient like I did Mrs. Roth, and she has
changed my life for the better in so many ways.

*****

Sheila, her soul sister for over 50 years, who thankfully chose Zel over Stuart, on Ronnie Sue, the friend:

We have gone through so many passages in
fifty years, as girls, as married women, as
mothers and grandmothers, as solo people,
and together suffering her illness and my
blindness for the last four or five years. Where
do we start? We have so many shared thoughts
and so many shared secrets and in so many
ways depended so totally on each other for so
many things. She tells me often that she keeps
telling the boys (Zel and Dad) she's not ready
yet; be patient...she'll be there soon enough. I
cannot even begin to imagine my life without
her.

*****

Lona, with whom Ronnie explored her love of the arts on every level, from arts-in-education programs to the Broadway stage. Lona and Ronnie, who had quickly adopted each other, spent many years developing a connection to one another's souls.

Lona, a "sister from another mister," on Ronnie Sue, the artist:

My dear, 'sistah' Ronnie...

What a life you have lived! And, though your physical being no longer walks this earth, you are with me, forever. You have managed to visit me often these last few weeks, reminding me of the things we would say, the places we would go and the people we have known and loved together. I will continue to talk to you forever.

Since 1994 (Rachel was 10, Rory was 5) my children knew you would play an important role in their lives—not just through your creative spirit and undying support, but with your heart. Know why? Because your heart is my heart; my heart, yours. And, your brother, Kip and my kids were the first to know that.

We are very different people. We related to the world in such different ways, yet somehow, we are the same.

*Your wisdom still gives me insights into the behavior of others, and I know my intellect offered you an honest appreciation for the realness of our world. My mission was to **always** give you an experience you might not* *have otherwise, to make our world together a larger place. And, you created numerous pathways to **always** make it happen.*

*We have walked hallways, alleyways, the streets of Broadway and have seen the grandeur of the arts in all forms—from the audience, from backstage, from the wings and in the galleries. We stood listening to new songs in our 'home studio,' then you would say, "Send that to me. I **need** to have that one." Your playlist grew dramatically with the original music Kip writes and Rory sings. We have listened to stories from modestly famous people who shared with us because of what we are—lovers, dreamers, givers...with the same artful heart.*

We have stood in my kitchen with the brisket roasting, and the pecan pie waiting, people arriving to join us, but we never skipped a beat; we could be interrupted, but never stopped in our thoughts, words, heartfelt feeling...with each other. We shared Thanksgiving after Thanksgiving—and so many other holidays eating, drinking and being merry (and recounting some unusual experiences with 'people' who don't think like we do). And (the best) just the two of us sitting at the table with wine and snacks, and I always had the White Zinfandel and a straw waiting for you. Mostly, then, you would stay for dinner... And my family, who are also your family, would weigh in.

*So many memories. So many shared words. So much to still have because of our sisterhood. People leave the earth, and those still here feel the loss. It's indescribable. But, as we have agreed on **many** occasions, artists are brave people; they put their very souls into the universe so that those who watch have their worlds changed forever because of the experience. You have been an artist of unique existence, my sistah. And my life is changed forever. So, you live. With the universe... In my heart.*

Loving you as always,

Lona

*****

Vinny, my dear high school friend, who not only connected with Chris and I in our youth, but with my parents as well as we grew into adulthood. Vinny, on Ronnie, the encourager:

There is no way in a brief space to express how fortunate I was to have Mrs. Roth be a part of my life. She was the ever happy, ever kind, free spirit that makes everyone feel welcome. I have many fond memories of spending time with her during my high school years and beyond. Hanging out at Mrs. Roth's house at night usually meant watching some TV with her and Stu while they relaxed in bed. We would all just pile in and hangout, talk and laugh. It was the most natural thing and she welcomed all of us with open arms. Each parent in our group of friends added something unique that made growing up easier. Mrs. Roth added her smile, support, laughter, and encouragement.

She also provided me with support to face my first big professional challenge as a CPA. I prepared Mrs. Roth's taxes and she was audited by the IRS. It was an in-person office audit. I told her no problem; I will take care of it. Well, it was the first audit I was ever on. I was terrified. No idea what to expect, no idea what to do and I was worried that she was going to pay more in taxes, penalties, etc. As I met with her to put the paperwork together, I was confident, smiling and very sure of myself (on the outside at least). Inside I was a hot mess and very unsure of myself.

We finished the paperwork, and I was scheduled the next day for the audit. Before I left, she gave me a big hug, looked at me and told me I was going to do great, to be confident and she believed in me. She pretty much looked right through the tough exterior I was faking and talked to that high school kid who grew up with her. In thinking about her words of encouragement, it occurred to me that she was not just talking about succeeding on the audit but that she wanted me to face the challenge and learn from it, whatever the outcome. It was exactly the encouragement and support I needed to put the fear aside and to face this situation head on. As I deal with the IRS on a regular basis now, my mind does roam back to that first audit and that hug and her words of encouragement. Oh, and by the way, she won the audit and even got more money back from the IRS! Cha-ching!

As she was nearing the end of her journey with us, she was able to tell Stacey stories of her life, both the highs and devastating lows. In telling these stories, she gave me another gift of encouragement and gratitude which I will never forget. The loss of Stu (the only one of the parents I call by their first name by the way because, well, he was Stu!) was the most life changing. At that time, she asked me to take a look at her finances to get things in order and make sure that she was going to be okay. I was happy to be of assistance to her in whatever way I could. She mentioned to Stacey that this really gave her peace of mind at her most low.

I am grateful that I was able to help, but in reality, I was only paying the favor back to her for all the years of laughter, encouragement, and support. I will miss her terribly but am grateful that she (and Stu) were part of my life.

*****

I must take this opportunity to talk for a moment about a very special individual. Her name is Victoria, and she was Mom's hospice nurse who saw her through the last few days of her life. She was extremely good at her job—comforting with hugs when I broke down, gentle and direct with knowledge when it was required. She let me know what I needed to do to be okay with helping her through the end of her life.

On her first visit on Wednesday, Mom still had some level of consciousness. Victoria examined her, then listened to her breathing, which was very shallow. She said it was close; that the most important thing we could do was to say everything we needed to tell her. Mom needed to know that it was okay for her to let go; to have permission to leave this earth. Victoria explained that sometimes, people at the end of their lives hold on because they are worried about their loved ones and whether they are going to be okay when they are gone. I spent the next two days telling her just that.

Victoria witnessed firsthand the magic of Ronnie that Wednesday. As she was sliding into a semi-comatose state, we did FaceTime calls with Chris, my girls, and Judy. There were tearful goodbyes, and proclamations of love, and Mom would open her eyes and try to engage with whomever was on the screen. She was able to converse a little, murmuring, "I love you" as she lifted a finger and listened to everyone say how much they loved her and how special she was. When we hung up, she'd fall back asleep, or whatever resting state she was in. I do wonder what thoughts she had with each interaction with the ones she loved most.

What Victoria later explained was how when a dying person is surrounded by love, they will go to extraordinary lengths to come to consciousness to respond. They will expend an exorbitant amount of energy to do so, out of a deep, deep sense of love and caring. Even with death approaching, Ronnie Sue loved her family so much that she wanted everybody to know that she was still present in mind and paying attention, even if on the surface it didn't seem that way.

Victoria also suggested that since the sense of hearing was the last thing to go, it might be good to play her favorite music. On Thursday, as I sat with her, I started picking random songs from YouTube of artists she loved—Barbra Streisand, Andrea Bocelli, The Mormon Tabernacle Choir. I also felt compelled to play "Because You Loved Me" by Celine Dion because every word still applied just like it did when we danced to it at my wedding. I played songs that I had recorded over the summer for Facebook entertainment and sang to her live (she always loved hearing me sing). Eventually, I got her iPad and started playing her playlists. Whatever I could do to distract her from the rapid breakdown her body was experiencing, I tried.

I didn't sleep much that Thursday night. I kept waking up suddenly and checking on her. Based on her breathing pattern, I kept watching her to see if the next breath would be the last one. She kept going. I couldn't fathom how she was sustaining life with those shallow breaths. I even tried mimicking the pattern and it was so uncomfortable...and she was doing it with one working lung.

Friday morning, Victoria came to visit and check on Mom, and she said that the end was very close. It would be "today or tomorrow." Based on her physical examination, she admitted that she couldn't understand how Mom was still hanging on and said that there may be some people she needed to hear from. I sort of scrambled because all of the family members had gotten their chances to say goodbye to her on FaceTime messages. However, there were two very important people in her life that she hadn't yet heard from.

I immediately texted Lona and Sheila and told them that Mom needed to hear from them. She needed them to tell her that it was okay to go. My mother heard their sweet, calm, familiar voices tell her that it was time for her to finally rest. I also called Chris, who my mother adored and always listened to what he had to say. He had told me that after he initially said goodbye on Wednesday, he realized there were so many other things that he still wanted to say. I called him and told him that this would be his chance. I put him on speaker, and he so bravely and confidently told her that it was time to go, she had done her job, that she had lived her life well, that he would always take care of me and the girls, and that she could now finally be at peace.

I am eternally grateful for Victoria's support, compassion, and guidance. It is a gift I can never repay her. I was by Mom's side holding the hand that looked just like mine until her last breath. I watched, waited, and assisted however I could. In her last moments, I took stock in her features, her skin, her hair...knowing that soon, I'd only have the memory of her. I took solace in the notion that I was there, watching her take her last breaths, ushering her soul into the universe. In the flash of a moment, her soul was released, making her way to Daddy in the clouds.

Things Ronnie Loved

Surround yourself with beautiful things.
Life has a lot of grey and sadness—look for
that rainbow and frame it.

~ Charlotte Kitley

No matter what, Mom always smelled like vanilla; always like she just walked out of a bakery. When I was growing up, her fragrance of choice was Shalimar, which is what my childhood mind associates with her. Now, it happens to be my fragrance of choice. When I wear it, and it gets in my clothing, I bury my nose in my collar and think of her. But somewhere along the line she made a switch to pure vanilla spray. I even remember her once when she was baking; she dabbed a little vanilla extract behind her ears. She always smelled welcoming, and when you hugged her, you were embraced not only by her arms, but by the warm sweetness of her smell.

Somehow, the things Mom touched were always beautiful. Her ability to execute her creative vision with a craftsmanship was second to none. Beaded petit-point pictures and pillows reflecting her artistic and cultural interests were her specialty. She made a giant portrait of King Tutankhamun with tiny beads and gold thread that she mounted in a gold and black floating frame that was to die for. Another masterpiece was a depiction of the movie poster for "Gone with The Wind." I now have both of these pieces in my home.

Mom had the most beautiful cursive handwriting—something I always wished I could emulate but was always too lazy to practice. She hand-wrote all of the addresses on our wedding invitation envelopes in her own Ronnie-calligraphy. Even her sloppy, scratch handwriting was gorgeous. In the spring after she passed, I found an envelope with a spa gift certificate she had given me back in 2019. She had written, "I love you, Mommy" on it. I finally used the gift, but kept the certificate, just so I can look at her handwriting.

Knitting was also one of her special talents. She was extremely skilled at it and made it look sort of cool. When I was a kid, she would knit sweaters with different styles, patterns, and textures. She made her outfit for my Bat Mitzvah where she knit giant, sparkly sequins, one by one, into the pattern. She made a sleeveless sweater with the queen of hearts intricately depicted on the entire front. In the last year of her cancer struggle, she got bored often, and binge-watching Netflix shows wasn't cutting it. I suggested that she should pick up the knitting needles again and create something. She got busy planning out her pattern and started casting on her stitches. Soon enough, I received a purple infinity scarf that keeps my neck warm in the winter, a pair of leg warmers for when I teach dance, and scarves and blankets for the girls to cozy up to. She was insanely talented and even with the handicap of chemo brain and increasing neuropathy in her hands, her muscle memory took over and her needles were clicking away again. I'd often get proud texts with progress pictures.

Growing up, I remember Mom being an avid reader. She'd devour anything about English history and royalty (she obsessed over Princess Diana), Abraham Lincoln, American history, Ancient Egypt, Grey's Anatomy (the medical encyclopedia and much later, the TV show), Thomas Jefferson (the Paris years) and the Sally Hemmings lineage, Louis XIV, and FDR—pretty much most historical figures with big accomplishments. She was fascinated by people who did great things with less technology than what we have today. She had an affinity for the Vanderbilts and their "summer cottages" in Rhode Island. She marveled at how they knew to build massive homes with labor who lived on the property.

Her passion for music reached far and wide; she loved listening to beautiful instrumentalists and vocalists who performed show tunes, pop, and classical music. Elvis Presley, The Mormon Tabernacle Choir, Mandy Patinkin, Barbra Streisand, The Canadian Tenors, Josh Groban, Pentatonix, Collabro, the soundtrack of 1776, The Greatest Showman, and Andre Rieu are just a tiny fraction of the artists she loved to listen to. If the music was rich, powerful, and harmonic, she listened to it. When Lin-Manuel Miranda's "Hamilton" came out, Chris and I were obsessed with it. I thought Mom would love it, given her penchant for musicals and American history. I told her to give it a listen, and at first, she balked because it was largely a rap musical, and she thought she wouldn't be able to understand it. When she finally relented and listened to the score, she too became obsessed. She would listen to it on a loop in the house, in the car...wherever she went.

Mom's tchotchkes reigned in our home. Carousel horses could be found in all sizes and shapes. When I was young, she and her friend Janet refinished a real carousel horse that sat at the foot of her bed for years. They also made porcelain dolls together and Mom acquired several Madame Alexander collectibles. While she couldn't keep real orchids alive, she always had beautiful silk ones in her room. Through the years, she filled her curio cabinets with Swarovski crystal figurines, many of which wound up back in my house with my daughters. Family was so important to her, and since she always had loved ones who lived far away, she surrounded herself with pictures of them in fancy frames.

Whenever possible, there would be fringe or glitter in her life. She earned the moniker "Miss Glitza" when we worked in the flower shop. Her signature flair was sprinkling fine glitter all over the finished arrangement so that it shimmered when you walked past it. Mom's wardrobe was filled with things that sparkled and loved anything with fringe. Maybe living in Houston connected her to the cowboy spirit, and along with the fringe, she had quite a collection of fancy cowboy boots and hats.

Art she was drawn to was Erte's women, Degas dancers, and Monet's Garden paintings. She loved looking at beauty as seen through the eyes of these artists. She collected a plethora of coffee table books with pictures about her passions. When we cleaned out her room, there were stacks of huge coffee table books to be donated.

Mom had images of Fleur de Lis everywhere. I always thought it had something to do with having lived on Fleur de Lis Drive, but actually, being from New Orleans, she was immersed in historical French culture, and it was the symbol of France. She loved the shape, and she surrounded herself with the image.

Mom loved my Chris and my Chris loved her. It was a mutual admiration society from when we were teenagers. The one thing they had in common that had *nothing* to do with me was talking about the law. She always had a fire and desire to get into topical discussions on all things legal. Throughout most of my relationship with Chris, when they started talking about law, my eyes glazed over and my attention waned, but I marveled at how animated and interested she was—sometimes for hours. Chris was all too happy to oblige because he saw how much it entertained her to engage him in the thing he knew most about. They had a connection with each other that I was so proud of and grateful for, even when I lost interest in the subject being discussed and either found something else to focus on, or drifted off for a nice nap.

Finally, Mom adored her grandchildren and never wanted them to see her in a way that was "not herself" or upsetting. Ever the protector, she wanted them to be wearing the rose-colored glasses when it came to their memory of her. Even with me, when we weren't in each other's physical presence, Mom didn't want me to worry or feel badly for her.

Ronnie Sue loved anything that we accomplished. She would kvell over the little things and the big things; whatever activities we did or accomplishments we made, she was always impressed and awestruck. She saw most of the shows I was in or had produced as a director, and I'd always get an excited email with lots of exclamation points and expressions of pride in all caps. I think she just loved seeing the next generations thrive and always took great interest in hearing about the projects into which we poured our hearts and minds. She marveled at the glory of seeing her grandchildren grow up. We are all her legacy; we carry on the lessons she modeled, just by living her magnificent life.

Now What?

*What we have once enjoyed deeply we can
never lose.
A sunset, a mountain bathed in moonlight,
the ocean in calm and in storm—
we see these, love their beauty, hold the
vision to our hearts.
All that we love deeply becomes part of us.*

~ Helen Keller, *We Bereaved*

After Mom reunited with Dad, I understood that I had some serious healing to do. I knew I didn't quite understand the depth of sorrow I felt yet, but I knew it was just a matter of time before that became clear. There were boxes of her stuff in my garage that made their way to my house before I even returned home. I pulled into the garage from the airport and as the door opened, they were there, waiting for me. A wave of shock overcame me as I parked, and I had to pause for a moment, thinking, n*ow what*. These are the boxes I had to open, sort through, cry over, and find a way to insert the contents into my already crowded home. Just like she surrounded herself with the stuff she loved, I felt compelled to surround myself with some of those things. I needed to be able to look around and see those things that remind me of her, even at the risk of triggering sudden tears. Eventually the tears would fade.

In the few days before the funeral, I slept in the guest room, aka *Nanny's Room*. The main reason was because at that time in the COVID-19 pandemic of 2020, New York State still had a mandatory 14-day quarantine for anyone who was traveling from states with elevated virus rates. Since Texas was one of those states, I knew going in that I'd have to be isolated, but I also knew that I may not get another chance to be with her. It was a "now or never" decision. The secondary reason, one that I am actually grateful to the quarantine for, is that I got to spend some time in the room where Mom slept happily whenever she visited me. I hung her favorite black, bedazzled cowboy hat above the bed—the one with the RSR rhinestone pin on the front, along with her sparkly baseball caps, one of which I bought for her during one of her many hospital stays. She had been losing her hair and I wanted to give her something fun to cover her head.

Nanny's room became a retreat when I experienced a wave of emotions. It was a place I would speak to friends, spend time with Chris and the girls, cry, and laugh. A friend of mine had sent me a book that I started to read, and from the window behind me, a geometric heart of light shined on the open page. I was wondering when Ronnie was going to send me a sign. People always talk about seeing butterflies or feathers. I saw a light reflection of a heart. That seemed appropriate, Ronnie Sue. Thank you.

I believe the process of grieving is to reframe your mental process when thinking about a person; they go from someone who "is" to someone who "was." When that person is a parent, you have to find a way to retrieve the part of your soul that was sucked out of you the moment they passed. When you find it, you have to shove it back into your being, even though it doesn't quite fit the same way it used to.

We spent that Labor Day Monday resting, for the most part. Chris brought up four of the boxes I had shipped home, and the four of us unwrapped the miles of bubble wrap to reveal all of Nanny's stuff. We looked at old photo albums and Ronnie's high school yearbook, and we marveled at the plethora of evidence of how schools were still segregated in 1965. I wondered what was going on in Ronnie Sue's mind while all of that civil unrest was happening throughout the country.

We unwrapped sterling silver pieces, and some crystal pieces, and some old chinaware that didn't survive the trip.

The beaded handbags, scarves, and Nanny's decorated caps now had a new home. We touched everything, together as a family. Sophie collected all the bubble wrap and later spent the evening watching her videos and popping bubbles on her bed. That mountain of bubble wrap stayed in her room for months. Eventually, I started looking at things for work, since the next day would start professional development for a virtual school setting. I decided I would attend the first day of meetings because it was time to start focusing on the future. Ronnie Sue wouldn't have wanted it any other way.

*****

The funeral was tough. About twenty-five friends and family came, masks on, to celebrate Ronnie's life. I would imagine, if it weren't for COVID-19, we'd have had many more people there, sharing their heartfelt memories of her. But even with people sharing from home over Zoom, the ceremony was simple and perfect. When the hearse arrived, I had to identify Mom since she had traveled from Houston to New York, and they needed to make sure they had the correct person. It was one last glimpse of the shell that once held her soul. For a moment, I yearned to hold her hand one more time.

The Monday before, when I spoke with my girls about the service, I asked them if they wanted to speak about Nanny.

Sophie passed but amazingly, Julia was interested. Julia also had the idea to sprinkle glitter on the grave, since "Nanny always sparkled." Stroke of genius, and completely apropos for Miss Glitza. The rabbi said she had never seen glitter sprinkled on a grave, but she liked the idea very much, so a glittery grave we would have.

Part of the ceremony of a Jewish funeral is for the family and friends to shovel dirt into the grave. It's a *mitzvah*, a good deed, and very honorable. Like at my father's funeral, I was the first to shovel. Then, my girls followed, then Chris and then the rest of the crowd. That first sound of the dirt hitting the pine coffin is unique, hollow, and startling. Then seeing the crowd line up one by one to participate in this emotionally difficult task overwhelmed us. However, the thing that raised our spirits was opening up the little zipper bag of glitter and sprinkling it all over the dirt. We each took a turn, and the mood changed a bit. Everyone understood. I think it gave everyone a little cheer. A few people rushed up to take a turn, and for a moment, the sadness lifted as we all shared in the secret of the glitz.

I'm so proud of my girls. We held and squeezed each other. Julia got hit in waves of emotion, as did I, and Sophie was mostly quiet and shed a small tear towards the end. The four of us held each other when things got particularly tough.

When it was time for eulogies, Julia bravely stepped forward and spoke loudly and clearly...

> *Anyone who knew my grandmother, knew she loved glittery, bright objects. I remember as a kid I was always fascinated by them. She always had a new piece of jewelry or a new trinket with a story and I would sit with her and listen as she regaled me with the tale of said piece. Her face would always light up and her voice would get higher, and we'd sit there talking. I was always so fond of her visits, not just because I love her, but because she was such a fascinating woman, and anyone who knew her would agree.*

> *Only as I aged did I realize how much she was like the gems and stones she held so dear—like a diamond, bright and strong. She could light up a room with her presence even at the very end. Her positivity and kindness radiated out of her; you could catch a smile even on the darkest of days.*

> *Not only was she a radiant person; she was also one of the strongest women I have ever known. Not many could go through all she had and come out with a smile and a chuckle. She was an inspiration; she taught me how to look on the lighter side and appreciate the world for*

all its wondrous beauty and not become heavy with its misery.

We have lost a brilliant beam of pure light in this world, and while it is a tragedy, I will carry on her legacy by being kind, looking at the positive aspects of life, and dousing myself in glitter.

I had the honor of delivering my father's eulogy, and now, I would deliver the same honor for my mother. Some excerpts...

Today, we come to celebrate the fantastic life of Ronnie Sue Roth. It is impossible to adequately express the impact that she had on this world. She was a devoted daughter, wife, mother, sister, and friend. She held her loved ones close to her heart and had a few hand-picked people who she embraced with her soul...

When my father died, Mom not only lost the love of her life, but she suddenly became a single parent...No matter what was needed, whether it was direct, hands-on support or giving the space to figure out problems, Mom was always there standing in the wings. She was always ready to voice her opinion if needed, or just stopped to listen when I needed to vent. She was a confidante to anyone who needed her, and always gave good counsel....

The most important thing to her was being secure in the knowledge that we were going to be okay. As the recipient of her devotion to her family, I learned exactly what to do in order to support her in her time of need. She knew that the love and connection you give, you get back a hundred-fold...and she gave a lot of love to the world...

Ronnie was a fighter, with a demure grace that endeared everyone she met. Crossing her was never a good idea, and if she thought you were wrong, she let you know it in no uncertain terms. But, she always made it easy to be in her corner, and she knew that even if she disagreed with you, being kind and respectful was always more important than any semantic point she was trying to make...

Mom's strength played out in her fierce battle with cancer. When she was diagnosed, she prepared herself for a fight over the long haul. Her goal was to live. For nearly four years, Ronnie endured major surgeries, chemotherapy treatments, poking and prodding and every kind of test imaginable. She beat the odds over and over again with each anniversary of survival and being taken down easily was just not something Ronnie would tolerate. Her intention was to live as long as possible to continue to enjoy her family, her work, and spend as much time on this earth as possible...

My mother loved the law. From the time she was twenty until just a few weeks shy of her passing, Mom always worked for law firms. She reveled in legal research and writing, and often engaged my husband Chris in lengthy discussions about legal minutiae that would make my eyes glaze over every single time a lively discussion broke out about contracts or constitutional law, or whatever topic du jour happened to crop up. This kind of personal passion was the model...Whatever you do, you put your whole self into it. Immerse yourself in every aspect of your passion and strive to be the best version of you while doing it. That is what makes for a life well-lived...

Mom conducted herself with honesty, integrity and character, every single day of her beautiful life. Whether through work, or her twenty-five years volunteering for Coupé and Rockland Youth Dance Ensemble, or anything she chose to pour herself into, Ronnie made her environment, and the people in it, better for her efforts. She embraced Chris with open arms, welcoming him without question into the family. Her grandchildren saw first-hand the magic of their Nanny as she showered them with her love and light. Even in the end, when it was hard for Ronnie to muster the energy to stay awake, whenever the kids were in her presence, a switch was flipped, and she would shine just a little brighter for them. Again, it was always about protecting and loving her family.

It is hard to fathom this life without Ronnie Sue. My mom was my idol, my model, my friend, and my first love. She taught me everything I needed to know to reach out into the world and spread light and love. When I look at my hands, I think of her. When I smile, I see her.

When God made Ronnie Sue, she smashed the mold. I live each day working to make her proud of me, and to know that in raising me, she did good, because she was good. Mom, you did good. Now it's time to play with Daddy again. They are together, just above us, dancing on the clouds.

As the crowd dispersed and we said our thankful goodbyes, I started to walk away. Realizing I had one more thing to do, I ran back, found a rock, and placed it on the family headstone. This is where my paternal grandparents, and now both my parents, are buried. The rock is a symbol that someone they loved was there.

We headed back to the car, drained, and drove away. I was content to have kept my promise to Ronnie Sue that I would take care of her and get her to rest with Daddy. Now, she was finally at peace.

I had a moment on the drive home. I had the sudden urge to text Mom to let her know how proud I was of the girls, and how I know they will be okay; how they were honorable and provided support to their emotional mother as they grieved themselves in their own ways. It was one of those spontaneous thoughts that I would normally have picked up my phone and started typing. This is the moment that I was talking about earlier—the reconciliation of "is" to "was." It will have to suffice that instead, I turn my thoughts upward, send those mental messages to the ether, and hope that I see a random heart of light as I move through the rest of my days without my mom walking this Earth.

*****

As the days and weeks slipped by, I worked to insert myself back into "normal life." Of course, the definition of normal had changed drastically in so many ways. The world was still amidst the effects of the COVID-19 pandemic. Our schools started in a remote fashion, so every ounce of mental energy at work was spent trying to re-define what teaching classes and having rehearsals looked like. I suppose it provided a necessary distraction and respite from the emptiness and sadness I felt as I dealt with the rolling memory that Ronnie Sue no longer walked this earth. That was the second drastic change. Before, even though I didn't speak with her every day, I knew that at any time I could call her number or text an emoji to her and when she was awake, she'd respond right away—or at least when she woke up from her nap. She would do her best to put her bright, shiny self in the forefront and chatter in my ear about all the little things she experienced, the gratitude she felt for her blessings, and sometimes the struggles she was having. I could blather on about my projects, my frustrations, or my moments of parental pride. I was always mindful that I should enjoy the opportunity I had to talk to her because I knew it wouldn't be there forever.

Now, the moments that I had dreaded are here. When I want to share something, she is no longer a phone call away. I must now send those thoughts out into the universe and imagine how she would have responded. While it does make me sad, it is in those moments when I reflect on the last week that I was blessed to spend with her. I was able to tell her what I needed to say and also what she needed to hear.

For now, and for the rest of my days, I am content with the knowledge that I will always carry that last week in my soul.

*****

One night, in early October, I took out my faded red Cancun t-shirt. I use it as a sleep shirt. The weekend I spent with Mom at Dana and Stephen's wedding in Mexico, she had bought one for each of us just as something fun we could share. She put mine on my bed and when I arrived it was a cute surprise. Without thinking, I took the shirt out of my drawer and got ready to put it on, when I got a pang. I realized she was gone. Again. That happens every so often. A wave of reality hits when another life experience happens. Your usual mental framing of the situation shifts, when you think about how the different people in your life might have some effect on your perspective on the situation, and you remember that someone significant is no longer there. It is a quiet, insidious realization that slowly builds until one day you crack, and the emotion flows like lava.

Then, two days before my birthday (the first one without her), images and thoughts kept flooding my head of our trips, the last week we spent together, and for the first time in many weeks, I broke down and cried. The memories found a chink in the armor and split it wide open. I yearned to see a birthday text or see her name appear on my phone when she called. She was always so enthusiastic about birthdays and always sent a gift to commemorate another year. All of those things were not going to happen this year, and the child in me got very, very sad.

Sometimes, a day or two goes by, and I don't think about it much. Then, I'll get a wave of an unsettling thought: *Mom isn't here anymore. She doesn't exist on this earth anymore. I can't touch her, talk to her, or listen to her respond. I can't make her laugh or tell her a story that will invite her to give me some advice. I can't tell her how the girls are doing and hear how encouraged she is by their progress. I can't vent to her about work or share some lovely happenstance that occurred.* Of course, people say you can always talk to her now, and I sometimes do, but her physical eternal absence is just...unsettling, discombobulating, sad. I'm still not used to thinking of her in the past tense—don't know if I ever will, to be honest.

I wear her jewelry, look at her pictures and her stuff and I realize it's all just remnants of the past—things she left behind. It's the same empty feeling that was there when she was removed from her room the day she passed. That feeling was further cemented when I looked at her that last time when her body arrived at the cemetery. When the funeral director opened the casket, it was her; I recognized the shell and remembered what she looked like when she breathed, smiled, slept, laughed. In my mind, I tried to see her breathing, rosier, fuller. But the reality was clear; it was time to say goodbye to seeing her for the last time.

The funeral director asked me if I needed a few moments alone with her, and I quietly declined. He secured the coffin and in the short trip that I accompanied her to her final resting place, I felt the responsibility, the weight, the finality of the moment. She would be appropriately memorialized before her friends and family. Chris and I would embrace our children and usher them through Ronnie's end-of-life rite of passage.

It is hard to think that now, both of my parents are gone. While I am a "fully-formed adult" with my own family, career and generally happy life, the child in me longs for her parents—the one that never got to know me as an adult, and the one who lovingly ushered me into my adult life. I am far from "on my own," but I now have to move forward only with the thought, *What would Ronnie Sue have said? What emojis would she send if I sent her a text?* I now live with a hint of sadness in perpetuity. That is the fluid experience of grief that lives just under the surface.

Of course, this kind of sadness would immediately be met by her with "turnaround talk"...ways to look at things in a brighter light, ways to distract me from the sadness and redirect me to a more level place. When I was growing up, Mom was often labeled as seeing the world through rose-colored glasses, as though that somehow deterred or distracted her from processing the harsh reality of life, but really, I think she was just a "grateful for life" sort of gal. There would always be setbacks, and she would always work through them.

Wallowing in self-pity or sorrow wasn't her style, and while she wasn't unsympathetic to my feelings, it was definitely hard for her to hear that we were struggling. She always wanted us to be okay and I think she tried to model that for us. For the most part, I think I carried that lesson with me. While I do sometimes get stuck in the thoughts of the challenges that come from the things I cannot control, the things I'm desperate to change, I have developed a mindfulness that the challenges are temporary. I learned from Ronnie that there are more pressing and important thoughts into which you can and should pour your mental energy. So, just when I start to go down a dark path that threatens my ability to move forward, I acknowledge the source of my sadness, and then I create. I organize. I connect. I hug my family. I remember how Mom pressed on through every challenge she faced, great and small, and I try to follow her lead.

Life is too short to stop for too long and allow yourself to get swallowed by sadness. There are so many ways to revive your happiness, to center yourself and to move forward. I will always miss her. I will always yearn to talk to her and hold her hand. I will always miss her jubilant texts filled with Bitmojis and ALL CAPS, especially on my birthday. I will always be grateful that I was chosen by the universe to be her daughter, to learn from her, and to teach her lessons to my children. For every step I take, I will always look to what Ronnie Sue knew to help me find my way.

I am honored to be the daughter of sparkling Ronnie Sue. She chose Stuart Barry and together, they created me. From now on, every action I take will have their memory in mind. I will continue to work to honor them and make them proud and now, I can feel their embrace giving me the strength to stretch myself a little further than ever before. I can take solace in living each day with the lessons that Ronnie Sue knew. Now, I live a full life of joy, surrounded by people who I care about, doing things I believe in, because Ronnie Sue and Stuart Barry loved me.

When I need to feel their embrace, I can wrap my arms around the people I love and give away a little bit of their essence because it lives in me every day. I can look in the eyes of those who knew them and connect to a part of them embedded in others. I can impart upon my children a foundation of the gifts of love and wisdom my parents bestowed upon me, as seen through my eyes. That, I believe, is the lens within which I envision the rest of my life from this point forward. I do so with gratitude.

Thank you, Ronnie Sue and Stuart, for leaving your love in our hearts and becoming a part of us for all eternity.

Afterword

Cancer sucks.

~ me

L ong story short, by now you know this story deals with Mom's nearly four-year battle with cancer. As I was looking for inspirational quotes for this chapter, I just couldn't find one that felt right. Cancer just sucks. Of course, you want to be positive, inspirational, and motivational for the patient, so they continue their fight to hopefully slay the unmerciful beast. While they are still breathing, there is a chance to survive, perhaps to thrive, and to bank some more time. Looking back, you can be proud of their fight and try to pull some iota of good from the experience. But make no mistake...Cancer sucks. Anyone who has had the experience, whether fighting it themselves or supporting a loved one, can attest to that.

From her peritoneal cancer diagnosis late in 2016 forward, I saw Mom in many different states of health—from vibrant and spunky to leaning on death's door. For every slide, she slowly climbed her way back. Her will to live was impenetrable. Death was an unacceptable option and she wanted to be a survivor. She endured hospital stays, surgeries, procedures, chemotherapy—all to give her as much time as possible on God's green earth and spend it loving on her family.

My role in the cancer mix was typically as the "drop and run" person. Since I lived in New York, it was impossible for me to raise my family, work full-time and be in Houston to care for her with any regularity. Mom was there, happily ensconced in her space, binge-watching her favorite Netflix shows, knitting, spending time with family and working remotely for Charles and Lucille. While there were some visits that were geared towards fun and traipsing around town with her—to Tiffany's nail salon, to devour beignets and crepes at Javaman, and to run all sorts of mundane errands—most were in response to some dire health crisis. The shock of a sudden emergency hospitalization would shift me into a different mode: I'd get things covered at home and work, buy a ticket, arrange for someone to pick me up from the airport, and *go*. Literally. My husband and daughters, thankfully, always understood and managed to keep things running smoothly at home. Each time I'd arrive at her door, the look on Mom's face washed away any sadness, stress or anger I may have felt towards the situation. Occasionally, I'd just show up at her bedside. She would take a look at me, do a double take in disbelief, and cry in relief and joy.

This last time was no different. When I arrived in her doorway, and she warbled *'you're really here,'* I hugged her gently, sat by her side and held her hand the rest of the night. I knew I made the right decision. We needed to see each other.

Once I settled into her bed next to her, we started chatting. I opened my laptop and instead of focusing on work-related things while she slept, I decided now would be a good time to write down as many of the random stories my memory refused to retain as she had the energy to tell. As I started asking her questions, she dictated her story, and I typed furiously. The sound of my fingers on the keyboard reminded me of her nails clicking on hers for so many years. Among her many talents, she was a gifted typist, and I was just hoping that I would be able to type as fast as she could to capture everything she had to say. She seemed to like the idea that she was being interviewed about her life and talked with vigor and animation until she ran out of energy, then fell asleep. As the oxygen tank whirred on, she took shallow breaths that sustained her through the night.

When I called home and told my family what I was doing, my daughter Julia made fun of me, telling me I should just record her "on the device called a phone" (smartass), but I wanted to get Mom's thoughts on the screen in real time as she spoke; I wanted to make sense and order of all the puzzle pieces I had wondered about over the years and try to fit them all together. If there was a hole, I could stop and try to redirect her to fill in the blank. It was a marvelous engagement with the history that was locked in her brain, and an opportunity I didn't want to squander. I love my mom so dearly, and I wanted to hold on to more than the tchotchkes and possessions that she loved. They are nice and having them helps me to connect to her to a point, but I wanted to know more about who she was, where she came from and how we got to this point in time.

What's funny is that even as exhausted as she was, Ronnie Sue's mind was still pretty sharp. She was very animated as she told the history of her parents and my dad and her perception of things about life. I have no idea how accurate every detail of every story is, but it all came from her and how she perceived the events she described. She became excited to wake up from her long naps and give me more to type. I think she appreciated the idea that her story will live on in some way. I'd re-read and organize her thoughts, as she rested next to me, breathing shallowly, and I waited for the next window of opportunity so I could squeeze just a little more of Ronnie Sue's essence onto the page.

What was amazing about writing this memoir, even through the challenges of many edits and re-writes, was the cathartic nature of dealing with my ongoing grief of losing her as it unfolded over time. Reading her words, remembering our shared history, learning a little more about her than I already knew, made it a little bit easier to bear because it is a permanent chronicle of some of her history, our relationship and how her extraordinary life impacted mine.

To me, there is no one else who is as dear and magical a being as my mom. While it pains me to think of her as not being here anymore, I am content with the notion that she set me up for life. I am a good, kind, loving person because of her. I try to spread that love all around with every person I encounter. I have a strong work ethic and devotion to my family. I want her to be proud of me, and I know she was because she told me that. Often... In ALL CAPS.

This book is my tribute to one of a kind; my gift is to share a little bit of her essence with the rest of the world.

Love you, Mom.

Mom and Me in Naples

With All My Love,
Mommy

Artwork by Serena Hubert

Also by Stacey Tirro

On May 25, 2020, amidst the viral pandemic that shut the world down, George Floyd was murdered in Minneapolis, Minnesota by an arresting officer when he kneeled on Mr. Floyd's neck for nearly nine minutes. For many people throughout our nation, and in our local communities, this was a breaking point. Patience and hope crumbled as protests escalated. Wounds that were already open were further torn apart by more violence and destruction. People of color, and their allies, expressed their disbelief, exhaustion and sadness over the fact that more than fifty years has passed since the Civil Rights Act, and we are still fighting for equal and fair treatment in our society. *How Do We Feel Right Now* is a collection of those narratives - real-time responses often expressed through social media - in the days and weeks following the tragedy. It is also an expression of the allyship that is being forged and the work that still needs to be done. Intended for theatrical production, *How Do We Feel Right Now* elucidates and educates communities about the ongoing struggles still expressed by people of color.

Available on Amazon Books

About the Author

Stacey Tirro is a dance, theatre, and fitness educator at Spring Valley High School and the author of the play *How Do We Feel Right Now? A collection of raw thoughts in the aftermath of senseless tragedy*, which her students of Thespian Troupe 721 produced virtually in December 2020. Her work has been highlighted in *American Theatre Magazine, Theatrefolk, The Unsealed, Strong Women Project Magazine,* and *Erika's Lighthouse.* Her first memoir, *What Ronnie Sue Knew,* is a loving tribute to the life lessons learned from her mom and dad that enabled her to follow her heart throughout her life. Her podcast, *A Moment of Mindful Meditation,* is available wherever you listen to podcasts. Stacey lives in New York with her husband, Chris, and her daughters, Julia and Sophia. Find out more at her website staceytirro.com.